VOYAGE TO GOA AND BACK

(1583 - 1592)

VOYAGE TO GOA AND BACK

(1583 - 1592)

WITH HIS ACCOUNT OF THE EAST INDIES
(From Linschoten's Discourse of Voyages, in 1598)

Jan Huyghen Van Linschoten

GYAN

Published by

Gyan Publishing House
5, Ansari Road
Daryaganj, New Delhi-110002
Phone: 011-47034999, 9811692060
E-mail: books@gyanbooks.com

Distribution Network
gyanbooks.com
India, USA, Canada, UK, Australia, France

ISBN : 978-81-212-4209-7 (PB)
First Published, West Minister, 1903

2nd Impression 2020

Printed at: Gyan Press, Delhi.

Voyage to Goa and Back
1583 - 1592
Author: Jan Huyghen Van Linschoten

AN ENGLISH GARNER

VOYAGES AND TRAVELS

mainly during the 16th and 17th Centuries

VOL. II

WITH AN INTRODUCTION BY

C. RAYMOND BEAZLEY, F.R.G.S.

FELLOW OF MERTON COLLEGE, OXFORD

Author of *The Dawn of Modern Geography*

WESTMINSTER

ARCHIBALD CONSTABLE AND CO., LTD.

1903

PUBLISHERS' NOTE

THE texts contained in the present volume are reprinted with very slight alterations from the *English Garner* issued in eight volumes (1877-1890, London, 8vo) by Professor Arber, whose name is sufficient guarantee for the accurate collation of the texts with the rare originals, the old spelling being in most cases carefully modernised. The contents of the original *Garner* have been rearranged and now for the first time classified, under the general editorial supervision of Mr. Thomas Seccombe. Certain lacunae have been filled by the interpolation of fresh matter. The Introductions are wholly new and have been written specially for this issue.

CONTENTS TO VOLUME II.

INTRODUCTION TO VOLUME II

THE second volume of these travels opens with an abridgment of the first part of the celebrated *Itinerario* of Jan Huygen van Linschoten—'John the son of Hugh,' from the village of Linschoten in Utrecht, the probable home of his forefathers, but not his own birthplace. The author was born at Haarlem in or about 1563; in 1573, either before or just after the great siege of Haarlem, by the Duke of Alva, the family removed to Enkhuizen in North Holland, a town which escaped the Spanish re-conquest. At the age of sixteen, on December 6, 1576, young Jan started on his travels, and his first objective was remarkable. It was the country with which his countrymen, and especially the city of Enkhuizen and the province of North Holland, were so desperately struggling. Political war co-existed with an active commerce, and Linschoten sailed from the Texel in a fleet of some eighty vessels, bound for San Lucar in Andalusia. After a stay of six years in Spain (as the narrative tells us), mainly in Seville and Lisbon, Jan sought employment in the East Indian fleet, like his half-brother Willem Tin, who went in the same ship as *schrevijn* or *clerk* (not *purser*, as in the English translation, vol. ii. p. 7, etc.). Shortly after Linschoten's arrival at Goa, on September 21, 1583, John Newberie, Ralph Fitch, William Leedes, and James Storey were brought there under arrest from Ormuz, accused of being spies in the pay of Don Antonio, pretender to the crown of Portugal.[1] Drake's voyages in the Pacific and East

[1] For Linschoten's account of this, see vol. i. pp. 324-30.

Indies were of recent occurrence, and Englishmen were now regarded as somewhat of a dubious blessing in the Portuguese East. It was therefore with difficulty that Linschoten, his friend and comrade Bernard Burcherts of Hamburg, and Thomas Stevens the Jesuit, procured the release of Newberie, Fitch, and the other Englishmen. In 1584 Burcherts returned to Europe by the Persian Gulf, the Euphrates, and Aleppo; but Linschoten remained, hoping vainly for an opportunity of extending his travels to Eastern Asia. China and Japan, he wrote to his parents, were about the same distance as Portugal from the Malabar coast, a three years' journey: a Dutch friend of Linschoten's, one Dirck Gerritsz, had just been to the Far East as a gunner, and had pressed him to go too. In those distant and favoured lands two hundred ducats might easily be turned into six or seven hundred; but the necessary capital was wanting. Gerritsz, nicknamed 'the Chinaman' from his China voyages, was born at Enkhuizen, and spent in all twenty-six years in the Indies. He returned in the same ship with Linschoten, which sailed from Cochin on January 20, 1589; and from him comes most of the information of the *Itinerario* about the navigation of the China seas. In 1598 he piloted the Dutch fleet on its first voyage by the South-West Passage (of Magellan's Straits) to India. His notes on India are occasionally embedded in Linschoten; but their only proper edition was in Lucas Jansz Waghenaer's *Thresoor der Zeevaert* (Leyden, 1592). The *Itinerario* of Linschoten, as we have suggested, contains the results, not only of Linschoten's own experience, but of that of many other travellers; and the author, it is clear, was a collector of Hakluytian industry and judgment. He appears to have been hard at work upon it from the time of his return to Enkhuizen (September 3,

1592) until the complete publication of this encyclopædic survey of 'Cape Commerce' and 'Cape Routes' in the beginning of 1596. On October 8, 1594, the States-General of Holland granted him a formal licence to publish, but the book was not then ready, although parts of it seem to have been informally circulated, and all its chief suggestions were known to and discussed among the leaders of Dutch commerce during 1595.

In compiling his great book Linschoten was greatly helped by the eminent scholar, Bernard ten Broecke, the physician of Enkhuizen, who in the world of letters was known as *Paludanus*, the Latin equivalent of his surname, for scholars were still ashamed to be known as John Brewer and Jim Baker. Many of the notes and not a few passages interpolated into the text are from the hand of Paludanus, whose comments, though learned enough, are not always as much in touch with fact and nature as could be desired.

The *Itinerario* is divided into three principal books or parts, the first containing the narrative of the journey proper, in ninety-nine chapters, running to six hundred and twenty-seven pages in the Hakluyt Society's (1885) reprint of the English translation of 1598. In the second part (the first to be published, in 1595) is a collection of the routes from Europe to East and West Indies alike, in many cases translated from unpublished manuscripts of Portuguese and Spanish pilots; here is also an abundant mass of notes on the routes of the China seas. This part of Linschoten's work had great political importance; it served as the chief guide to the Dutch fleets in their early expeditions to the East, and in their first attempts to wrest the mastery of the Indies from Spain and Portugal. In the third part we have a brief description of the East and West coasts of Africa and a fuller account of America, mostly taken from earlier writers, such as Lopez on the Congo; Jean de Lery on Brazil; Peter Martyr and Oviedo on America in general. The *Itinerario* was originally illustrated by thirty-six maps, plans, and copperplate illustrations; in the Old English version of 1598 there are twenty-one topographical plates and thirty-two portraits and views. The world-map in the Dutch edition professes to be by J. Bapt. Vrient of Antwerp, famous as the publisher who bought the *Atlas* of Ortelius, and brought out an enlarged edition of the same. In the English edition the *mappe-monde* has the title *Orbis terrarum typus de integro multis in locis emendatus, Auctore Petro Plancio*, 1594; and in the left-hand corner, below the figure called *Mexicana*, is the inscription *Ioannes a Duetecum* [i.e. Doetechum] *junior fecit.* The other maps, in the English edition, include one of South-east Africa and part of the Indian Ocean, one of Western and Southern Asia from Egypt to Aracan (*imprinted at London by John Wolfe, graven by Robert Beckit*), one of Indo-China and the East Indian Archipelago, one of South Africa (*graven by William Rogers*), one of all Africa except the western hump, one of South America, one of South-western Africa and the Atlantic, one of Madagascar or St. Lawrence Island, one of Sumatra, one of Java Major, one of the Congo region, four of St. Helena (an engraved map and three profiles), one of Goa by Linschoten himself, one of Angra in Terceira (Azores), one of the two hemispheres (in small scale), and one of Spain.[1] From the resolutions of the States-General of Holland it appears that in 1592 Cornelius

[1] See De Jonge, *De opkomst van het Nederl. gezag in O. India*, vol. i. pp. 167-9; Tiele, intro. to Hak. Soc. ed. of Linschoten, pp. xvii-xix, xxx-xxxiii.

Claesz of Amsterdam, the printer and publisher of the *Itinerario*, aided by Peter Plancius, obtained a collection of sea-charts and routiers from Bartolommeo de Lasso, cosmographer to the King of Spain. The States gave Claesz a patent for printing and publishing not only the aforesaid, but also a *mappe-monde* or *land and sea-chart of the world*, drawn by Plancius and engraved by Joannes a Doetechum, as well as a chart of Asia made by an expert in the art of navigation at Goa in East India. The world-map of the *Itinerario* appears to be a reduced copy of the above-mentioned *mappe-monde* of Plancius; and extensive loans from De Lasso's collection are apparent in several of the sea-charts in Linschoten's work.

After his return from the East, Linschoten took part in the Dutch Arctic voyages of 1594 and 1595. In 1595 the first Dutch fleet sailed for the 'Indies of the Orient,' and we know from the journals of the expedition that the *Itinerario* was of the utmost value as a guide and directory. The second part of the same, comprising the Nautical Directory and Routes for the Indian and China seas, was already published (as we have pointed out) in 1595, and was greatly used on board the ships of this fleet; much also of the most important matter in the first part had been orally communicated to the leaders of the venture; and it is clear that the course of the voyage beyond the Cape of Good Hope and its special direction upon Java was due to the suggestions of Linschoten, who promised his countrymen a practical monopoly of the Java trade, 'for that the Portingales come not thither.'

In 1598 Linschoten (now settled in Enkhuizen for good) published a Dutch version of the great treatise of the Jesuit Acosta on Spanish America (*Historia natural y moral de las*

Indias), a work which he praises as far superior to the American sections of the third part of his own *Itinerario*; and in the same year Lucas Jansz Waghenaer in the preface to his new *Enkhuizen Zeekaertboek* thanks Linschoten for his help in the same, based on material derived from his northern voyages. In 1610 our traveller petitioned the States-General—unsuccessfully—for a pension; he did not long survive this rebuff; on the 8th February 1611 he died, at the very early age of forty-eight.

The *Itinerario* is one of the most valuable travel-records ever published, not only for its own subject-matter, but because it revealed to Holland and to other rivals of Spain and Portugal how weak the Eastern Empire of Philip II. really was. It thus played a most important part in exciting these rivals to active hostility in the East Indies, to the vigorous and persistent carrying out of what Drake had threatened in 1579, and Cavendish in 1587. As its political importance was speedily recognised, it soon met with readers out of the Netherlands. The famous old English translation (as well as a German) was published in 1598; two Latin versions appeared in 1599, and a French translation in 1610.

The English edition, here in part reprinted, is anonymous, but in the title to the second part (*The true and perfect description of . . . Guinea . . .*) W. P. (William Phillip?) is styled the translator. The version here given is loose, periphrastic, and super-abundant, constantly introducing words which are not in the original, and are not always warranted by the original. It also misses not infrequently the exact meaning of technical terms. On the whole, nevertheless, it gives a good broad view of all that Linschoten has to say, though it requires checking in details.

The notes of Paladanus, both in and out of the text, are omitted in the present reprint, which also abridges the text in many places,[1] and omits practically the whole of Linschoten's lengthy description of Indian lands, manners, markets, products, peoples, fauna and flora, extending from chapter v. to chapter xcii., from vol. i. p. 43 to vol. ii. p. 158 in the Hakluyt Society's edition of the complete Old English translation (1596-1885; see pp. 1-126 of this volume).[2]

Passing by the next two tracts, both relating to the destruction of Spanish and Portuguese Carracks in 1592-4 by English seamen (see vol. ii. pp. 129-150), we come to the *Miserable Captivity of Richard Hasleton* (pp. 151-180), originally printed in 1595, under the title *Strange and Wonderful Things happened to Rd. Hasleton, born at Braintree in Essex, in his ten years' travels in many foreign countries.* This is illustrated by various cuts, said to be taken from Poliphilo. The scene on p. 157, where Hasleton, urged to take the cross into his hand, spits in the inquisitor's face, is very typical; not less so is the protest on p. 168, 'Can any man which understandeth the absurd blindness and wilful ignorance of the Spanish tyrants, or Romish monsters, think them to be of the true Church? which defend their faith with fire, sword, and hellish torments.' . . . In

[1] *E.g.* pp. 3, 14, 15, 16, 17, 18, 19, 21, vol. ii. of the present collection.

[2] Much has been written, and more conjectured, about early Portuguese knowledge of the interior of Africa, the great lakes, the Nile sources, etc. A valuable hint as to this is afforded by a passage in Linschoten, Hak. Soc. edn., i. 31; this is omitted in our present reprint, but properly occurs after the words *mine named Monomotapa* on p. 17 of vol. ii.: 'in the which land is a great lake out of which you may perceive the river Nilus to spring forth, as likewise the great and wide river of Cuama or Niger [Quilimane? *i.e.* Zambesi], which runneth between Sofala and Mozambique into the sea. This, taken in connection with the Pigafetta map of 1591, may well be thought to prove a remarkable though unsifted and often vague knowledge of Upland Africa among the sixteenth century Portuguese.

Hasleton, even better than in Phillips or Hartop, we have the perfect prototype of Salvation Yeo.

Hakluyt's note (pp. 182-5) on the antiquity of English trade in the Levant, which follows, traces this East Mediterranean commerce or 'Turkey Trade,' grown to such importance under Elizabeth, from the early years of Henry VIII. (1511, 1512, etc.); while the voyage of the Earl of Cumberland, in 1589, to the Azores (pp. 186-212) forms an interesting chapter in the English counter-stroke after the ruin of the Spanish Armada of 1588; just as the fight of the *Dolphin* against five Turkish men-of-war, off Cagliari in Sardinia, in 1616, is a typical episode in the constant struggle of Mediterranean trade against Moslem piracy (see vol. ii. pp. 213-220). The Battle of Lepanto had scotched but not killed the snake: Europe was not finally freed from Mohammedan pirates until the French conquest of Algiers in 1830, though during the seventeenth century the nuisance was reduced to small dimensions.

Edward Wright, the annalist of Lord Cumberland's 1589 voyage, was the greatest scientific geographer of Elizabethan England. He was born about 1558, at Garveston in Norfolk, and became a Fellow of Caius, Cambridge, in 1587, soon after which he devoted himself to the study of navigation as a branch of mathematics. His most famous work, *Certain Errors in Navigation*, was published in 1599, and in 1614 he was appointed Lecturer in Navigation to the East India Company. He died in 1615, having won the position of the 'English Mercator' by his emended form of the famous projection of Gerard Kaufmann ('Mercator'), originally published in 1556. The present narrative is extracted from *Certain Errors in Navigation* (cf. also Purchas's *Pilgrimes*, iv. 1142-4, ed. of 1625).

Sir Francis Drake revived (see vol. ii. pp. 221-294) is an account of the so-called 'third' West Indian voyage of the great leader, that of 1572-3 to the Spanish Main. The region of Tierra Firme, or Golden Castille, then formed part, officially, of the Province of Hispaniola (Española), whose capital was at San Domingo. Since the discovery of the Peruvian silver mines in 1545, its ports had acquired immense importance as the points from which most of the treasure was shipped to Europe. We have already met with Drake in connection with the Hawkins voyages; it may be well to add here that he was born at Crowndale, near Tavistock, in Devonshire, in or about 1545; and made his first voyage to the West Indies with Captain Lovell in 1565-6, his second American voyage with Hawkins in the disastrous venture of 1567-8, his third (so far as known) in 1570, his fourth in 1571. The expedition of 1572-3 was in reality, therefore, his fifth to the New World. All the three latter claimed to be (as we are told in *Drake revived*; see vol. ii. p. 228) voyages of revenge, attempts to pay back to Spain the personal injuries received at Rio de la Hacha in his first venture, and at San Juan de Ulua ('Ulloa') in his second. They were also probably intended as diversions in the larger political struggle of England and Elizabeth against the Counter-Reformation, which assumed so acute a form in 1569-70.

As pirates, filibusters, and leviers of private war in the West Indies, Drake and the other English raiders of this time were preceded by French Huguenots, who sacked Havana as far back as 1536, and since that time had made incessant attacks upon the Spanish-American settlements of the Atlantic seaboard, until their success emboldened them to attempt a permanent colonisation within the Spanish sphere of interest in Florida (1565).[1]

The only account of Drake's raid of 1570 is in a paper of Spanish origin (*A Summary Relation of the Robberies done by Fr. Drake*), which describes it as accomplished by a vessel of only forty tons, captained by Drake ('with whom there went a merchant of Exeter called Rich. Dennys'). The same authority declares 'upon the coast of Nombre de Dios they did rob divers barks in the river Chagres that were transporting merchandise of 40,000 ducats of velvets and taffetas, . . . besides gold and silver in other barks.'

The voyage of 1571 was almost equally 'rich and gainful,' and it was now that Drake discovered his 'Port Pheasant,' probably the 'Puerto Escondido' or 'Hidden Haven' of the Spaniards, about four leagues south-west of the modern 'Caledonian Bay,' in the Gulf of Darien (see vol. ii. p. 229, etc.). The capacities of this as a base for future attacks upon the Spanish Main he saw at once, and in *Drake revived* the extreme importance of the position is apparent throughout. According to Lope de Vega,[2] the English captain (supposed to speak excellent Spanish) had visited Nombre de Dios disguised as a Spaniard; and his accurate knowledge of the topography in 1572 may be taken as some proof of the story of the *Dragontea*. Now also Drake gained a thorough knowledge of the treasure route from Peru to Panama, and across the isthmus to Nombre de Dios, where ships bound for Spain waited for their cargo.

To seize these treasures was clearly lawful for a true

[1] Just as in the same generation they attempted under Coligny's inspiration to plant themselves within the Portuguese sphere in Brazil (1558).

[2] *Dragontea*, canto i. On the other hand, it is disputed whether Drake as yet spoke Spanish at all.

Protestant hater of Spain, whether his country were or were not in a state of formal war with Philip II. Drake had it from the chaplain of his own ship that he might justly recover his losses (of 1566 and 1568) from those who had injured him; in fact, the 'case was clear in sea divinity, and few are such infidels as not to believe doctrines which make for their profit.'[1]

The spring of 1572, in which began the voyage whose story we have in *Drake revived*,[2] saw the start of a number of French and English vessels, half-traders, half-privateers, for Spanish America,—some twenty from Havre, at least two (besides Drake himself) from England. One of these was under James Ranse or Raunce,[3] probably the former master of the *William and John* in Hawkins' last voyage; the other was captained by John Garrett, probably the master of the *Minion* which escaped with such difficulty from the San Juan de Ulua fight in the venture of 1567-8. Raunce joined Drake off the Spanish Main a little later in this same year (see vol. ii. pp. 232-3); Garrett left

[1] Fuller, *Holy State*, p. 124 (ed. of 1648).

[2] Froude (*English Seamen*, pp. 108-9; ed. of 1895) is the only person who has challenged the authenticity of *Sir Francis Drake revived*, without any adequate reasons given or apparently forthcoming. The value of this booklet is of the first order; from it we derive almost all our knowledge of Drake's early feats in the West Indies and Spanish Main. From the dedication to Elizabeth, dated January 1, 1592-3, and written by Sir Francis himself, it would look as if, according to Court custom, he had presented the manuscript to the queen as a New Year's gift (cf. Corbett, *Drake*, i. 422).

Spanish versions of this expedition, strikingly confirmatory of *Drake revived*, may be found in the Record Office Manuscript 'Spanish State Papers,' xviii., of January 1580, called *Memoria de los Cossarios Ingleses que han hecho robas en las Indias*. In this paper the names of various owners of shipping captured or destroyed by Drake are given, along with a fairly minute account of the other English depredations. We may also cf. Hakluyt's extract from the *Discourse of Lopez Vaz, a Portugal*, and Duro, *Armada española*, ii. 506.

[3] Also spelt Rause or Rouse.

a warning for him at Port Pheasant that his hiding-place had been discovered (see vol. ii. p. 230).

All these ventures—Drake's, Raunce's, and Garrett's—appear to have had powerful backing: one authority[1] makes Drake the partner of Wynter and Hawkins. It is clear that behind him was a powerful group of navy men, merchants, and even statesmen, and that his little squadron was admirably fitted out, not for the execution of an irregular and independent freebooting scheme, but rather for one that needed the best equipment that England could give.

The 'Cimaroons,' Drake's native allies, who play so large a part in the narrative, were descendants of escaped negroes and 'Indian' women whom the Spaniards called 'Cimarones' or 'Hill-folk,' and the English sailors 'Maroons,' a name of pleasantly confused idea.

It has well been pointed out[2] that the nature and proportion of the arms served out to the landing party which attacked, took, but failed to hold Nombre de Dios, prove 'the action not of a mere pirate arming his desperadoes to the teeth, but of a man acquainted with the arrangement of a regular infantry *tertia*.' The absence of defensive armour was a concession to the incurable prejudice of English seamen in this matter, so much lamented by Sir Richard Hawkins,[3] so stoutly defended by others.

The great scene in the narrative (vol. ii. p. 269), where Drake gains his first view of the Pacific and prays for 'life

[1] The Ashmole Manuscripts referred to by Corbett, *Drake*, i. 159. On the other hand, Hawkins evidently felt bitterly about Drake's desertion of him after the disaster of 1568 (see note, p. 62).

[2] Cf. Corbett, *Drake*, i. 164-5.

[3] Cf. Rich. Hawkins's *Observations* (Hak. Soc. Ed.), pp. 302-4 (esp. 303-4), 'All men of good understanding, he declares, will condemn such desperate ignorance.'

and leave to sail once in an English ship in that sea,' has been justly seized upon by all who have studied Elizabethan history with any intelligence. It is indeed a decisive moment in the history of the English people as well as in the story of Drake's life: 'from that time forward his mind was pricked on continually night and day to perform his vow.'[1]

The French captain, Têtu of 'Newhaven' or Havre, who joined the English raiders on March 23, 1573 (see vol. ii. pp. 283-4, etc.), was perhaps the pilot Guillaume Le Testu of Françoise de Grâce, who published an atlas in 1555 which he dedicated to Coligny; the scimitar he gave Drake was a present from the Admiral of France, and (as our narrative says on p. 284) formerly belonged to 'Monsieur Strozze,' otherwise the Condottiere Strozzi.'[2]

Lastly, we may notice that the incident of the re-discovery and recovery of the buried treasure by the Spaniards (as mentioned in the narrative, vol. ii. p. 290) is confirmed in the *Dragontea* of Lope de Vega; just as the statement about the prizes taken (vol. ii. pp. 293-4) is borne out in general terms by the Spanish official complaint, which names several of Drake's captures, and adds that he took many other frigates engaged in the coasting trade of Tierra Firme and Veragua, with a great quantity of gold, silver, and merchandise. Among these prizes were a number of frigates newly built, at Havana and elsewhere, by the energy and skill of Pero Menendez de Aviles. For this terrible enemy of the Florida Huguenots was not merely a butcher of 'Lutherans' ('I do this not as to Frenchmen but as to heretics'), he was also the man who gradually equipped the Spanish Indies with some kind of defensive system, and to whom Philip II. owed the wisest

[1] Camden. [2] See Corbett, *Drake*, i. 190; Margry, *Navigations françaises*, 138-9.

advice he ever received from a subject in naval matters. It was with two of these new frigates that Drake and his company came home, and their merit is strikingly shown by the speed of the return voyage, which was accomplished in twenty-three days, from Cape San Antonio in Florida to the Scilly Isles (see vol. ii. pp. 293-4). Of the two vessels with which the 'Dragon' sailed from Plymouth, the *Pasha* was apparently abandoned at the close of the campaign: the scuttling of the original *Swan* is described on pp. 244-6.

Robert Knox's *Captivity in the Highlands of Ceylon* (1660-79), the last item in the present collection, is also the longest and one of the most interesting (see vol. ii. pp. 295-429). In the original edition of 1681 it has the title of *An Historical Relation of the Island of Ceylon in the East Indies, together with an Account of the detaining in captivity* [of] *the author*, etc.; there is a preface by Robert Hooke, M.D., who probably helped Knox to some extent in the polishing of his work. It is the earliest detailed account of Ceylon in English,[1] and by far the most valuable study of the interior which had been made in any European language up to this time. A Dutch translation appeared in 1692, a French one in 1693, a German in 1747. Robert Knox was born in 1640 or 1641, and lived till 1720. His father, a Scotsman of strong Puritan principles, had the same name as himself, and was, as we see from the narrative, a commander in the East India Company's service. He was made prisoner with his son and died on Feb. 9, 1660, leaving his unfortunate boy to grow to middle age in captivity. The latter, miserable as he usually was, employed his time admirably in observing and recording native customs, natural features, and recent Cinghalese

[1] Cf. vol. i. of Harris' *Navigantium Bibliotheca*, pp. 678, 811, 844, 938.

tradition After his escape he seems to have developed a morose temper and decided roughness of manner: his hatred of women was vehemently expressed in his letters: in Ceylon he rejects all offers of alliance with native females simply from the fear of thus increasing the difficulty of his escape.

Knox's captivity occurred during the long reign of Raja Singha II. (1635-85), the one hundred and seventy-second king since Vijaya, in B.C. 543, came from Palibothra on the Ganges to the sacred isle of *Lanka*.

'Ceylon was well known to the ancients under the name of Taprobane,' so every manual will tell us; but unquestionably under that name there is often a confusion between our Sumatra and Ceylon itself: both in Ptolemy (as 'Taprobane'), and in the *Periplus of the Erythraean Sea* (as 'Palaesimundus'), it appears as an island of gigantic size. Onesicritus and Megasthenes, Strabo and Pliny, all have something to say of Taprobane; under Claudius, Julian, Theodosius II., and Justinian, intercourse with the Roman Empire is recorded; and the names of Annius Plocamus in the first century, of Scholasticus in the fifth, of Sopater and Cosmas Indicopleustes in the sixth, have been preserved as those of visitors from the Mediterranean world to *Sielediva*. In the same way Fa Hien (*c.* A.D. 410) and Khi-nie (*c.* 970) made their way thither from the opposite end of the 'Habitable World'—from that 'Land of Han,' 'Celestial,' or 'Middle' Kingdom which had so close a bond with all centres of Buddhist faith, literature, and relic-treasure.

[1] In Ptolemy (*c.* A.D. 130) it is drawn as larger than Spain, and occupying most of the space that should have been given to the Indian Peninsula; in the *Periplus*, *c.* A.D. 90, it is described as of immense length, roughly like the shape of our Sumatra, but far greater, and bearing no perceptible resemblance to Ceylon.

Hiouen-Thsang (A.D. 628-649), however, the greatest of Chinese travellers, though he evidently longed to see the matchless jewels of Ceylon, did not touch there himself.

In the first half of the fifteenth century (1405-59), the island appears to have paid tribute to China, renewing then in more tangible form a shadowy allegiance of the earlier Middle Ages.

Among the Christian travellers[1] of the Mediæval Period who reached Southern and Eastern Asia, many refer to Ceylon, but few visited it, before the discovery of the ocean route round the Cape. Marco Polo and Bishop John de Marignolli are exceptions (*c.* A.D. 1293-4, and 1347-9). Even Nicolo Conti, though perhaps the first European to describe the cinnamon of *Seyllan*, does not seem to have landed (*c.* 1440).

On the other hand, the Arabs were constant visitors. Fa Hien found them there, two centuries before Mohammed. *Serendib* is one of the best-known points in the ninth and tenth century geography of Suleyman the merchant, Abu Zeyd Hassan, and Sindbad the Sailor; one of the clearest accounts of Ceylon before the advent of the Portuguese is that of the 'Doctor of Tangier,' Ibn Batuta (*c.* 1336 A.D.).

After Diego Cão, Bartholomew Diaz, Covilhão, and Vasco da Gama had opened the African or S.E. route to the Indies, an Italian trader, Girolamo di S. Stefano of Genoa, stayed a very short time in the island in 1498 or 1499. In 1506, the great traveller Ludovico di Varthema of Bologna, journeying by 'Arab' routes, touched at a port on the

[1] Friar Odoric of Pordenone, Bishop Jordanus of Columbum (Quilon), and John of Hesse are among the 'Latins' who wrote most fully of Seyllan or Sillan, but did not make a personal inspection.

west coast: as usual, he contrives to give more information in ten lines than most men in ten chapters.

The Portuguese knew Ceylon, as a coveted possession, from 1505, when under their boy-leader Lawrence or Lourenço, the hero son of the first Viceroy, Francisco de Almeyda, they attempted to gain a footing in the island, at Point de Galle. Affonso de Albuquerque (1509-15), as second Governor-General, seems to have meant to establish a fortress on some point of the coast; but the actual Portuguese dominion only began in 1517, when Lopo Soares de Albergaria appeared before Colombo and obtained permission to build a 'castle' there. The natives soon repented of their concession, and attacked the new settlement in force. Being vigorously repulsed, they acknowledged themselves, according to the conquerors' version, tributaries and vassals of the King of Portugal (see Camoens, *Lusiads*, x. 51). It is clear, however, that the people of the hilly upland struggled pretty successfully against the permanent extension of the Portuguese dominion. In 1542, and again in 1581, the dying rulers of 'Condé,' or Kandy, bequeathed their dominions to the Europeans, and in 1547-50 the Portuguese almost established themselves in the central fastnesses. In 1593-5 they did actually gain momentary possession of Kandy; and in 1560 they carried off and burnt the original tooth-relic of Buddha; but all these successes were transient. The Cinghalese refused to be willed away to foreign masters, and succeeded in repulsing each advance of their enemy, beyond the coastal lowlands. At the end of the sixteenth century, Linschoten (though perhaps with exaggeration) describes Colombo as the only real possession of the subjects of Philip II. in the island, 'which by mere force and great charges is maintained, for that they have no other place or piece of ground, no not one foot but that in all the land.' (See Linschoten, *Itinerario*, book i. chaps. xiii., xiv., xcii.). In 1587-8, Raja Singha I. fiercely but unsuccessfully attacked this 'small, strong, well-guarded' fort; and in 1595 the extreme barbarities of the would-be conqueror, Jerome de Azavedo, failed to crush the resistance of a people whom he drove to despair. Though he occupied Kandy, he could not make his raid produce any lasting results.

The Dutch paid their first visit to Ceylon in 1602; and between 1638 and 1658 they wholly expelled the Portuguese, substituting themselves as masters at Trincomali in 1639, at Point de Galle in 1640, at Colombo in 1656. Their timid and irresolute policy towards the native powers (as well as the studied cruelty of the Portuguese) is well brought out in Knox's narrative (see esp. ii. pp. 409-420). Here also is a very early notice of that vigorous onward movement of the French, which, in 1672, brought them from Madagascar, Bourbon, and the Isle de France to Ceylon and the Coromandel Coast, and which in spite of all discouragements continued apparently to prosper and progress till Dupleix made France for a moment (1742-50) the dominant power in the Deccan (see vol. ii. pp. 421-25).

The Cinghalese practice of detaining white visitors was not at all peculiar. Instances of it are common enough among semi-civilised nations: the most famous example, perhaps, is that of Abyssinia, where, to give only one instance among many, the first Portuguese envoy to the court of Prester John, Pero de Covilhão, was kept as a hostage to the day of his death (from 1490 to 1520).

C. RAYMOND BEAZLEY.

Oct. 24th, 1902.

JAN HUYGHEN VAN LINSCHOTEN.

Voyage, in a Portuguese carrack, to Goa, in 1583 A.D.

[*Discourse of Voyages &c.*, 1598.]

This celebrated Narrative of a journey to India and back (besides being an Eye Witness description of the economy of a Carrack) contains precise information respecting Portuguese affairs in India, at a time when the already enormous wealth of the Crown of Spain was being rendered almost omnipotent by the vast additional treasures brought to Lisbon in the yearly Fleet of Portuguese carracks : and also, at its close, gives us a large account of the splendid doings of the English fleets off the Azores, in 1589; including the last fight of the *Revenge*, and the dying speech of its Commander, Vice Admiral Sir RICHARD GRENVILLE.

BEING young and living idly in my native country, sometimes applying myself to the reading of histories and strange adventures, wherein I took no small delight; I found my mind so much addicted to see and travel into strange countries thereby to seek some adventure, that in the end to satisfy myself, I determined and was fully resolved, for a time, to leave my native country and my friends (although it grieved me); yet the hope I had to accomplish my desire together with the resolution taken, in the end, overcame my affection, and put me in good comfort to take the matter upon me; trusting in GOD, that He would further my intent.

Which done, being resolved, thereupon I took leave of my parents, who then dwelt at Enkhuisen; and being ready to embark myself, I went to a fleet of ships that as then lay before the Texel, staying for the wind to sail for Spain and Portugal: where I embarked myself in a ship that was bound for San Lucar de Barameda, being determined to travel unto Seville, where as then I had two brethren that had continued there certain years before; so to help myself the better, and by their means to know the manner and custom of those countries, as also to learn the Spanish tongue.

And the 6th of December in the year of our Lord 1576, we put out of the Texel, being in all about eighty ships; and set our course for Spain: and the 9th of the same month we passed between Dover and Calais.

Within three days after, we had sight of Cape Finisterre, and the 15th of the same month, we saw the land of Cintra otherwise called Cape Roca; from whence the river Tagus runneth into the main sea, upon the which river lieth the famous city of Lisbon: where some of our fleet put in, and left us.

The 17th day, we saw Cape St. Vincent; and upon Christmas day after, we entered into the river of San Lucar de Barameda; where I stayed two or three days, and then travelled to Seville. On the first day of January

[1577] following, I entered into the city, where I found one of my brethren; but the other was newly ridden to Court, lying, as then, at Madrid.

Although I had a special desire presently [*at once*] to travel farther; yet for want of the Spanish tongue, without the which men can hardly pass through the country, I was constrained to stay there to learn some part of their language.

In the meantime, it chanced that Don HENRY, the last King of Portugal died: by which means a great contention and debate happened as then in Portugal; by reason that the said King by his will and testament, made PHILIP [II.] King of Spain, his sister's son, lawful heir unto the Crown of Portugal. Notwithstanding the Portuguese—always deadly enemies to the Spaniards—were wholly against it, and elected for their King, Don ANTONIO, Prior of Ocrato, brother's son to the King that died before Don HENRY: which the King of Spain hearing, presently prepared himself in person to go into Portugal to receive the crown; sending before him the Duke of ALVA with a troop of men to cease their strife, and pacify the matter. So that, in the end, partly by force and partly by money, he brought the country under his subjection.

Whereupon divers men went out of Seville and other places into Portugal; as it is commonly seen that men are often addicted to changes and new alterations: among the which my brother, by other men's counsels, was one. First travelling to the borders of Spain, to a city called Badajos, standing on the frontiers of Portugal; where they hoped to find some better means: and they were no sooner arrived there, but that they heard news that all was quiet in Portugal, and the Don ANTONIO was driven out of the country; and PHILIP, by the consent of the land, received for King.

Whereupon my brother presently changed his mind of travelling to Portugal, and entered into service with an Ambassador that on the King's behalf was to go into Italy; with whom he rode: and arriving in Salamanca, he fell sick of a disease called *tabardilla* [*the spotted fever*], which at that time reigned [*raged*] throughout the whole country of Spain, whereof many thousands died; and amongst the rest, my brother was one.

Not long before, the plague was so great in Portugal, that, in two years space, there died in Lisbon to the number of 80,000 people. After which plague; the aforesaid disease ensued, which wrought great destruction throughout the whole country of Spain.

The 5th day of August in the same year, having some understanding in the Spanish tongue, I placed myself with a Dutch gentleman who had determined to travel into Portugal to see the country, and stayed with him, to take a more convenient time for my pretended [*intended*] voyage.

Upon the 1st of September following, we departed from Seville: and passing through divers towns and villages, within eight days after, we arrived at Badajos, where I found my other brother following the Court.

At the same time, died ANNE of Austria, Queen of Spain—sister to the Emperor RODOLPH [II.] and daughter to the Emperor MAXIMILIAN [II.]—the King's fourth and last wife; for whom great sorrow was made through all Spain. Her body was conveyed from Badajos to the Cloister of Saint Laurence in the Escorial; where, with great solemnity, it was buried.

We having stayed certain days in Badajos, departed from thence; and passed through a town called Elvas, about two or three miles off, being the first town in the kingdom of Portugal; for that between it and Badajos the borders of Spain and Portugal are limited.

From thence, we travelled into divers other places of Portugal, and at the last arrived at Lisbon, about the 20th of September following; where, at that time, we found the Duke of ALVA, as Governor there for the King of Spain: the whole city making great preparation for the coronation of the King, according to the custom of their country.

We being in Lisbon, through the change of air and the corruption of the country, I fell sick: and during my sickness was seven times let blood [*bled*]; yet, by GOD's help, I escaped.

Being recovered, not having much preferment under the gentleman, I left his service; and placed myself with a merchant, vntil I might attain to better means.

About the same time, the plague, not long before newly begun, began again to cease; for the which cause the King till then had deferred his entrance into Lisbon: which being wholly ceased; upon the first day of May, *anno* 1581, he entered with great triumph and magnificence into the city. Where, above all others, the Dutchmen had the best and greatest commendation for the beautiful shows: which were a gate and a bridge that stood upon the river side where the King must first pass as he went out of his galley to enter into the city; being beautified and adorned with many costly and excellent things most pleasant to behold. Every street and place within the city was hung with rich cloths of tapestry and arras: where they made great triumphs, as the manner is at all Princes' coronations.

The same year, the 12th of December, the Duke of ALVA died in Lisbon, in the King's palace; being High Steward of Spain: who, during his sickness, for fourteen days, received no sustenance but only women's milk. His body, being seared and spicen [*embalmed*], was conveyed into his country of Alva.

The same month, the King being yet at Lisbon, died Don DIEGO, Prince of SPAIN and PORTUGAL, the King's eldest son. His body being embalmed, was conveyed to Madrid. After whose death, the King had but one son named Don PHILIP, and two daughters living.

About the same time, there arrived at Lisbon, the King's sister, widow to the deceased Emperor MAXIMILIAN; and with her, one of her daughters, who being lame, was placed in a Monastery of Nuns. They with great triumph were likewise received into the city.

After the death of Don DIEGO, the King's eldest son, all the Lords and Estates of Spain and Portugal, as well spiritual as temporal, assembled at Lisbon, and there, in the King's presence, according to the ancient custom and manner of the country, took their oaths of faith [*fealty*] and allegiance unto Don PHILIP, the young Prince of SPAIN, and next heir and lawful successor of the King his father, in his dominions of Spain, Portugal, and other lands and countries.

The next year, *anno* 1582, a great navy of ships was prepared in Lisbon, whose General [*Admiral*] was the Marquis of SANTA CRUZ. He was accompanied with the principal gentlemen and captains, both of Spain and Portugal; who, at their own costs and charges therein, to show the great affection and desire they had to serve their Prince, sailed with the said Navy to the Flemish Isles [*the Azores*] to fight with Don ANTONIO; who lay about those isles with a fleet of Frenchmen, whose General [*Admiral*] was one PHILLIPO STROZZI.

These two fleets meeting together, fought most cruelly, to the great loss of both parts: yet in the end, Don ANTONIO with his Frenchmen were overthrown, and many of them taken prisoners. Among the which were divers gentlemen of great account in France: who, by the Marquis's commandment, were all beheaded on the island of St. Michael. The rest, being brought into Spain, were put into the galleys. Don ANTONIO escaped in a small ship; and the General STROZZI also, who being hurt in the battle, died of the same wound.

By this victory, the Spaniards were so proud, that great triumph was holden in Lisbon for the same; and the Marquis of SANTA CRUZ received therein with great joy.

Which done, and all things being pacified in Portugal, the King left his sister's son, Don ALBERTUS Cardinal of Austria, Governor of Lisbon and the whole country; and, with the Cardinal's mother, returned and kept Court at Madrid in Spain.

The beginning of my voyage into the East or Portuguese Indies.

STAYING at Lisbon, the trade of merchandise there not being great, by reason of the new and fresh disagreeing of the Spaniards and Portuguese; occasion was offered to accomplish my desire.

There was, at that time, in Lisbon, a monk of Saint Dominic's order, named Don Frey VINCENTE DE FONSECA, of a noble house: who, by reason of his great learning, had of long time been Chaplain unto SEBASTIAN, King of Portugal, and being with him in the battle in Barbary where King SEBASTIAN was slain, was taken prisoner, and from thence ransomed. Whose learning and good behaviour being known to the King of Spain, he made great account of him; placing him in his own chapel: and desiring to prefer him, the Archbishopric of all the Indies being void, with the confirmation of the Pope, he invested him therewith; although he refused to accept it, fearing the long and tedious travel he had to make thither. But in the end, through the King's persuasion, he took it upon him; with a promise, within four, or five years at the furthest, to recall him home again, and to give him a better place in Portugal: with the which promise he took the voyage upon him.

I, thinking upon my affairs, used all the means I could to get into his service, and with him to travel the voyage which I so much desired: which fell out as I would wish.

For my brother that followed the Court, had desired his master, who was one of His Majesty's Secretaries, to make him Purser in one of the ships that, the same year, should sail unto the East Indies: which pleased me well; forasmuch that his master was a great friend and acquaintance of the Archbishop's. By which means, with small intreaty, I was entertained in the Bishop's service; and, amongst the rest, my name was written down: we being in all forty persons.

And because my brother had his choice which ship he would be in, he chose the ship wherein the Archbishop sailed, the better for us to help each other: and, in this manner, we prepared ourselves to make our voyage.

There were in all five ships, of the burden of 1,400 or 1,500 tons each ship. Their names were, the admiral [*i.e., the flag ship*] *San Felipe*, the vice-admiral *San Jago*: these were two new ships, one bearing the name of the King, the other of his son. The other three were named the *San Lorenzo, San Francisco,* and our ship the *San Salvador*.

Upon the 8th of April, being Good Friday, in the year of our Lord 1583 (which commonly is the time when their ships set sail, within four or five days under or over), we, all together, issued out of the river of Lisbon and put to sea, setting our course for the island of Madeira: and so putting our trust in GOD (without whose favour and help we can do nothing, and all our actions are but vain) we sailed forwards.

The manner and order used in the ships in their Indian voyages.

THE ships are commonly charged with 400 or 500 men at the least; sometimes more, sometimes less, as there are soldiers and sailors to be found.

When they go out, they are but lightly laden with only certain pipes of wine and oil, and some small quantity of merchandise. Other things have they not, but ballast and victuals for the company. For the most and greatest ware that is commonly sent into India are Rials of Eight [=436 *reis* =5*s.* 9*d. then*=£1 14*s.* 6*d. now. The present Mexican dollar*]: because the principal Factors for Pepper do every year send a great quantity of money therewith to buy pepper; as also divers particular merchants, it being the least ware [*smallest in bulk*] that men can carry into India. So that in these Rials of Eight, they gain at least forty per cent.

When the ships are out of the river, and entered into the sea, all their men are mustered, as well sailors as soldiers; and such as are found absent and left on land, being registered in the books, are marked by the Purser, that at their return they may talk with their sureties (for that every man putteth in sureties): and the goods of such as are absent, being found in the ship, are presently brought forth and priced [*appraised*] and an inventory thereof being made, they are left to be disposed of at the Captain's pleasure. The like is done with the goods of those that die in the ship. But little cometh to the owner's hands, being embezzled and privily made away.

The Master and Pilot have for their whole voyage forth and home again, each man 120 Milreis[1] [=£80 *then*=£480

[1] The present Portuguese Milreis is a silver coin about 4*s.* 4½*d.* in value; and is roughly calculated at 4½ Milreis to the £1 sterling. But the Milreis referred to by LINSCHOTEN was a gold coin, and as such is quoted by JOHN MELLIS (at *p.* 155 of his edition of ROBERT RECORD's *Ground of Artes*, in 1586) among "the most usual gold coins throughout Christendom," as being worth 13*s.* 4*d.*

The Portuguese Ducat was Two-fifths of the Milreis, and would be, proportionately, 5*s.* 4*d.*; but LINSCHOTEN, at *p.* 459 of the original English edition of 1598, quotes it at 5*s.* 6*d.* We shall, however, for uniformity sake, herein take it (on MELLIS's equivalent of 13*s.* 4*d.* for Milreis) at 5*s.* 4*d.*: and in estimating for corresponding value in the present day, shall multiply by Six.

now] every Milreis [=13*s.* 4*d.*] being worth in Dutch money seven Guilders. And because the reckoning of Portuguese money is only in one sort of money called *Reis*—whereof 160 [=*roughly* 2*s. then*] are as much as a Keyser's Guilder or four [*Spanish*] Rials of Silver [*each=roughly* 40 *Reis*=6*d. then*]; so that two Reis are four Pence, and One Rei, is two Pence of Holland. I have thought it good to set it down the better to show and make you understand the accounts they use by Reis in the country of Portugal.

But returning to our matter, I say Master and the Pilot do receive beforehand each man 24,000 Reis [=24 *Milreis*=£16 *then*=£96 *now*]. Besides that, they have both chambers under in the ship and cabins above the hatches; as also "primage," and certain tons of freight. The like have all the other officers in the ship, according to their degrees; and although they receive money in hand, yet it costeth them more in gifts before they get their places; which are given by favour and goodwill of the *Proveador*, who is the Chief Officer of the Admiralty.

Yet there is no certain ordinance for their pay, for that it is daily altered: but let us reckon the pay which is commonly given, according to the ordinance and manner of our ship for that year.

The Chief Boatswain hath for his whole pay 50,000 Reis [=50 *Milreis*=£33 13*s.* 4*d. then*=£200 *now*], and receiveth 10,000 Reis [=10 *Milreis*=£6 13*s.* 4*d. then*=£40 *now*] in ready money.

The Guardian, that is the Quarter Master, hath 1,400 Reis [=18*s.* 8*d. then*=£5 12*s. now*] the month; and for freight, 2,800 [=£1 17*s.* 4*d. then*=£11 4*s. now*]; and receiveth 7,000 Reis [=7 *Milreis*=£4 13*s.* 4*d. then*=£28 *now*] in ready money.

The *Seto Piloto*, which is the Master's Mate, hath 1,200 Reis [=16*s. then*=£4 16*s. now*], which are three ducats [5*s.* 4*d. each*], the month; and as much freight as the Quarter Master.

Two Carpenters and two *Callafaren* [?] which help them, have, each man, four ducats [=£1 4*s. then*=£7 4*s. now*] a month and 3,900 Reis [=£2 12*s. then*=£15 12*s. now*] freight.

The Steward, that giveth out their meat and drink, and the *Merinho* [? *Master at Arms*] which is he that imprisoneth men aboard, and hath charge of all the ammunition and powder, with the delivering forth of the same, have each man a 1,100 Reis [=14*s.* 8*d. then*=£4 8*s. now*] a month and 2,340 Reis [=£1 11*s.* 2*d. then*=£9 7*s. now*] of freight; besides their chambers, and freedom from customs: as also all other officers, sailors, pikemen, shot [*harquebusiers*] etc. have, every man after the rate, and every one that serveth in the ship.

The Cooper hath three ducats [=16*s.* 0*d. then*=£4 16*s. now*] a month, and 3,900 Reis [=£2 12*s. then*=£15 12*s. now*] of freight.

Two *Strinceros* [?], those are they which hoist up the mainyard by a wheel, and let it down again with a wheel, as need is, have each 1,000 Reis [=13*s.* 4*d. then*=£4 *now*] the month, and 2,800 Reis [=£1 17*s.* 4*d. then*=£11 4*s. now*] of freight.

Thirty-three Sailors have each man 1,000 Reis [=13*s.* 4*d. then*=£4 *now*] the month, and 2,800 Reis [=£1 17*s.* 4*d. then*=£11 4*s. now*] freight.

Thirty-seven Rowers have each man 660 Reis [=8*s.* 9*d. then*=£2 12*s.* 6*d. now*] the month, and 1,860 Reis [=£1 4*s.* 9*d. then*=£7 8*s.* 6*d. now*] freight.

Four *Pagiens* [*Cabin boys*], which are boys, have with their freight, 443 Reis [=5*s.* 11*d. then*=£1 15*s.* 6*d. now*] the month.

One Master Gunner and eight under him, have each man a different pay: some more, some less.

The Surgeon likewise hath no certain pay.

The Factor and the Purser have no pay but only their chambers, that is below under the hatches a chamber of twenty pipes (for each man ten pipes) whereof they make great profit; and above the hatches each man his cabin to sleep in.

These are all the officers and other persons which sail in the ship, which have for their portion every day in victuals, each man alike, as well the greatest as the least, 1¾ lbs. of biscuit, half a can of wine, a can of water; and an *arroba*, which is 32 [English] pounds of salt flesh the month, and some dried fish. Onions and garlic are eaten in the beginning of the voyage, as being of small value. Other provisions as sugar, honey, raisins, prunes, rice and such like, are kept for those which are sick: yet they have but little thereof; for the officers keep it for themselves and spend it at their pleasure, not letting much go out of their fingers. As for the dressing of their meat, wood, pots, and pans; every man must make his own provision.

Besides all this, there is a Clerk and Steward for the King's soldiers that have their parts by themselves, as the sailors have.

This is the order and manner of their voyage when they sail into the Indies: but when they return again, they have no more but each man a portion of biscuit and water until they come to the Cape of Good Hope; and from thence home, they must find their own provisions.

The soldiers that are passengers, have nothing else but a free passage; that is room for a chest under the hatches, and a place for their bed in the orlop deck: and may not come away without the Viceroy's passport, and yet they must have been five years soldiers in the Indies before they can have licence. But the slaves must pay freight for their bodies and customs to the King; as in our voyage home again we will at large declare [*see pp.* 53-67].

Madeira to Mozambique.

THE 15th of April 1583, we espied the island of Madeira and Porto Santo; where the ships use [*are accustomed*] to separate themselves, each ship keeping on his course; that they may get before each other into India for their most advantage, and to dispatch the sooner: whereby, in the night and by tides, they leave each other's company; each following his own way.

The 24th of April, we fell upon the coast of Guinea, which beginneth at 9° N., and stretcheth until we come under the Equinoctial: where we have much thunder, lightning, and many showers of rain; with storms of wind which pass swiftly over and yet fall with such force, that at every shower we are forced to strike sail, and let the mainyard fall to the middle of the mast, and many times clean down, sometimes ten or twelve times every day. There we find a most extreme heat, so that all the water in the ship stinketh, whereby men are forced to stop their noses when they drink; but when we are past the Equinoctial it is good again.

The nearer we are unto the land, the more it stormeth, raineth, thundereth, and calmeth: so that most commonly the ships are at the least two months before they can pass the line. Then they find a wind which they name the "General Wind," and it is a south-east wind: but it is a side wind, and we must always be sideways in the wind almost until we come to the Cape of Good Hope.

And because that upon the coast of Brazil, about 18° S., lieth great flakes or shallows which the Portuguese call *abrashos*, that reach seventy miles into the sea on the right side; to pass them the ships hold up most unto the Coast of Guinea, and so pass the said flats.

Otherwise, if they fall too low or keep inwards, they are constrained to turn again into Portugal, and are many times in danger of being lost. As it happened to our admiral [*flagship*] *San Felipe:* which, in the year 1582, fell by night upon the flats, and was in great danger of being lost; yet recovered again, and sailed back to Portugal. And now, this year, to shun the flats, she kept so near the Coast of Guinea that by means of the great calms and rains, she was forced to drive up and down two months together, before she could pass the line; and came two months after the other ships into India. Therefore men must take heed and keep themselves from coming too near the coast to shun the calms and storms; and also not to hold too far off, thereby to pass the flats and shallows: wherein consisteth the whole Indian voyage.

The 15th of May, being about fifty miles northward of the Equinoctial line, we espied a French ship; which put us all in great fear, by reason that most of our men were sick, as it commonly happeneth in those countries through the exceeding heat; and further they are for the most part such as never have been at sea before that time, so that they are not yet able to do much. Yet we discharged certain great shot at him, wherewith (after he had played with us for a small time) he left us: so that presently we lost sight of him, wherewith our men were in better comfort.

The same day, about evening, we descried a great ship, which we judged to be of our fleet, as we afterwards perceived: for it made towards us to speak with us, and it was the *San Francisco*, wherewith we were glad.

The 26th of May, we passed the Equinoctial line, which runneth through the middle of the island of St. Thomas, by the coast of Guinea : and then we began to see the South Star and to loose the North Star, and found the sun at twelve of the clock at noon to be in the north. After that we had a south-east wind called a "General Wind," which in those parts bloweth all the year through.

The 29th of May, being Whitsunday, the ships of an ancient custom, do use to choose an Emperor among themselves, and to change all the Officers in the ship, and to hold a great feast which continueth three or four days together. Which we observing, chose an Emperor; and being at our banquet by means of certain words that passed out of some of their mouths, there fell great strife and contention among us: which proceeded so far that the tables were thrown down and lay on the ground [*decks*] and at the least a hundred rapiers were drawn—without respecting the Captain or any other; for he lay under foot and they trod upon him :—and had killed each other, and thereby had cast the ship away; if the Archbishop had not come out of his chamber among them, willing them to cease, wherewith they stayed their hands. Who presently commanded every man on pain of death, that all their rapiers, poniards, and other weapons should be brought into his chamber; which was done: whereby all things were pacified, the first and principal beginners being punished and laid in irons. By which means they were quiet.

The 12th of June, we passed beyond the aforesaid flats and shallows of Brazil, whereof all our men were exceeding glad: for thereby we were assured that we should not, for that time, put back to Portugal again: as many do. Then the "General Wind" served us until we came to the Rio de la Plata: where we got before the wind to the Cape of Good Hope.

The 20th of the same month, the *San Francisco* that so long had kept us company, was again out of sight.

The 11th of July after, our Master judged us to be about fifty miles from the Cape of Good Hope: wherefore he was desired by the Archbishop to keep in with the land that we might see the Cape. It was then misty weather, so that as we had made with the land one hour or more, we perceived land right before us and were within two miles thereof, which by reason of the dark and misty weather we could no sooner perceive: which put us in great fear, for our judgement was clean contrary; but the weather beginning to clear up, we knew the land. For it was a part or bank of the point called False Cape, which is about fifteen miles on the side of the Cape of Good Hope towards Mozambique.

The Cape of Good Hope lieth under 34° S. There we had a calm and fair weather, which continuing about half a day, we got with our lines great store of fish off the same land, in ten or twelve fathoms of water. It is an excellent fish, much like to haddocks. The Portuguese call them *pescados* [*i.e.*, *fishes*].

The 20th of the same month, we met again with the *San Francisco*, and spake with her; and so kept company together till the 24th of July, when we lost her again. The same day we struck all our sails because we had a contrary wind, and lay to for two days still driving up and down; not to lose any way. We were then against the high land of Natal; which beginneth in 32° and endeth in 30° S.

In this place they commonly use to take counsel of all the Officers of the ship, whether it is best for them to sail within or without the Island of Saint Lawrence [*Madagascar*]. For that within that land, they sail to Mozambique, and from thence to Goa; and sailing without it, they cannot come at Goa, by reason they fall down [*drift*] by means of the stream [*current*], and so must sail unto Cochin, which lieth 100 miles lower than [*south of*] Goa. It is as the ships leave the Cape, that it is or is not good to make towards Mozambique: because they cannot come in time to Goa by reason of the great calms that are within the island [*i.e.*, *of Madagascar*]. They that pass the Cape in the month of July may well go to Mozambique, because they have time enough to refresh themselves there, and to take in fresh water and other victuals; and so lie at anchor ten or twelve days together: but such as pass the Cape in the month of August, do come too late and must sail about towards Cochin, thereby to lose no time; yet it is dangerous and much more cumbersome, for that commonly they are sick of swollen legs, sore bellies, and other diseases.

The 30th of July, we were against the point of the cape called Cape Corrientes, which lieth under 24° S. There they begin to pass between the islands.

The 1st of August, we passed the flats called *Ox baixos dos India* that is "the flats of India" [now called *Bassa da India*], which are distant from Cape Corrientes, thirty miles; and lie between the island of Saint Lawrence and the firm land. There is great care to be taken lest men fall upon them; for they are very dangerous. Many ships have been lost there, and of late, *anno* 1585, a ship coming from Portugal, called the *San Jago* (being admiral [*flag-ship*] of the fleet; and was the same that, in its first voyage, went with us from Lisbon for vice admiral): as in another place we shall declare [*see p.* 30].

The 4th of August, we descried the land of Mozambique. The next day, we entered into the road, and as we entered, we espied the aforesaid ship, called the *San Jago,* which entered with us, not above one hour after we had descried it; being the first time we had seen it since it left us at the island of Madeira, where we separated ourselves.

There we likewise found two more of our ships, the *San Lorenzo* and the *San Francisco,* which, the day before, were come thither, with a small ship that was to sail to Malacca. Which ship commonly setteth out of Portugal a month before any of the ships do sail for India, only because they have a longer voyage to make: yet do they ordinarily sail to Mozambique to take in sweet water or fresh victuals, as their voyage falleth out or their victuals scanteth. If they go not thither, then they sail about the back [*i.e., the east*] side of the island of Saint Lawrence; not setting their course for the Mozambique.

There were now four of our fleet in company together, and only wanted the *San Felipe* which had held her course so near the coast of Guinea, the better to shun the flats of Brazil, that she was so much becalmed that she could not pass the Equinoctial line for a long time after us; neither yet the Cape of Good Hope without great storms and foul weather, as it ordinarily happeneth to those that come late thither: whereby she was compelled to compass about [*go outside Madagascar*] and came to Cochin about two months after we were all arrived at Goa; having passed through much foul weather and endured much misery, with sickness and diseases as swellings of the legs, the scorbutic, and pain in their bellies, etc

Mozambique.

MOZAMBIQUE is a little island distant about half a mile from the firm land: for the firm land on the north stretcheth further into the sea than it doth. The ships harbour so near to the island and the fortress of Mozambique, that they may throw a stone out of their ships upon the land. They lie between the island and the firm land, which are distant about half a mile from each other; so that they lie there as safely as in a river or haven. The island is about half a mile in compass, and is flat land bordered about with a white sand. Therein grow many Indian palms or [cocoa]nut trees, and some orange, apple, lemon, citron, and Indian fig trees: but other kinds of fruit which are common in India, are very scarce there. Corn with other grain, with rice and such necessary merchandise are brought thither out of India: but of beasts and fowls, as oxen, sheep, goats, swine, hens, etc., there is great abundance; and they are very good and cheap.

In the same island are found sheep of five quarters, for that their tails are so broad and thick, that there is as much flesh upon them as upon a quarter of their body; and they are so fat that men can hardly brook them. There are certain hens that are so black, both of feathers, flesh, and bones, that being sodden they seem as black as ink; yet of a very sweet taste, and are accounted better than the others: whereof some are likewise found in India, but not so many as in Mozambique.

Pork is there a very costly dish, and excellent fair and sweet flesh: and as by experience it is found that it far surpasseth all other flesh, so the sick are forbidden to eat any kind of flesh but only pork, because of the excellency thereof.

They have no sweet water in the island to drink, but they fetch it from the firm land: and they use in their houses great pots which come out of India to keep water in.

The Portuguese have therein a very fair and strong castle, which now about ten or twelve years past [*i.e., about* 1570] was fully finished: and it standeth right against the first of two uninhabited little islands, where the ships must come in, and is one of the best and strongest built of all the castles throughout the whole Indies: yet have they but small store of ordnance and ammunition. There are also no more soldiers than the Captain and his men that dwell therein: but when occasion serveth, the married Portuguese that dwell in the island, which are about forty or fifty at the most, are all bound to help to keep the Castle, for that the island hath no other defence than only that castle. The rest lieth open, and is a flat sand. Round about within the castle are certain cisterns made, which are always full of water: so that they have water continually in the same for the space of one whole year or more, as necessity requireth.

The government of the Portuguese in the island is in this manner.

They have every three years, a new Captain and a Factor for the King, with other Officers: which are all offices given and bestowed by the King of Portugal upon such as have served him in the Indian wars, in recompence of their services, every man according to his calling and degree: where they receive their pay and ordinary fees out of that which they get by force, for during their abode in those places, they do what pleaseth them.

The Captain hath great profit, for there is another fortress, named Sofala, towards the Cape of Good Hope. By that fort is a certain mine named Monomotapa where is great store of gold: and withal a certain kind of gold called by the Portuguese *botongoen onroempo* or "sandy gold;" for that it is very small, like sand, but the finest gold that can be found.

In this fortress of Sofala, the Captain of Mozambique hath a Factor; and twice or thrice every year, he sendeth certain boats, called *pangaios*, which sail along the shore to fetch gold and bring it to Mozambique. These *pangaios* are made of light planks and sewed together with cords, without any nails.

The Captain maketh the commodity of his place within the three years' space that he remaineth there: which amounteth to the value of 300,000 ducats [= £80,000 *then, or, about* £480,000 *now*], that is, nine tons of gold; as, while we were there, the Captain, named NUNO VELIO PEREIRA, himself showed us; and it is mostly in gold that cometh from Sofala and Monomotapa.

From Mozambique, they carry into India, gold, ambergris, ebony wood, ivory, and many slaves, both men and women, who are carried thither because they are the strongest Moors in all the East countries, to do their filthiest and hardest labour, wherein they only use them. They sail from thence into India but once every year, in the month of August till the half of September; because throughout the whole countries of India, they must sail with the monsoons.

Once every year, there goeth and cometh one ship for the Captain to India, that carrieth and bringeth his merchandise. No man may traffic from thence into India, but only those that dwell and are married in Mozambique. Such as are unmarried may not stay there, by special privilege from the King of Portugal granted to those that inhabit there, to the end the island should be peopled, and thereby kept and maintained.

Mozambique to Goa.

WE STAYED at Mozambique for the space of fifteen days, to provide fresh water and victuals for the supplying our wants. In the which time, divers of our men fell sick, and died by reason of the unaccustomed air of the place, which of itself is an unwholesome land; and has an evil air, by means of the great and unmeasurable heat.

The 20th of August, we set sail with all our company, that is our four ships of one fleet that came for Portugal; and a ship for the Captain of Mozambique whose three years were then finished. His name was Don PEDRO DE CASTRO; in whose place the aforesaid NUNO VELIO PEREIRA was then come.

The said Captain Don PEDRO returned with his wife and family again into India. For the King's commandment and and ordinance is, that after the expiration of their three years' office, they must yet stay three years more in India at the commandment of the Viceroy of India, in the King's service, at their own charges, before they may return into Portugal; unless they bring a special patent from the King, that after they have continued three years in their office they may return into Portugal again: which is very seldom seen, unless it be by special favour. Likewise no man may travel out of India, unless he has the Viceroy's passport; and without it, they are not suffered to pass, for it is very narrowly looked into.

The 24th August, in the morning, we descried the two Comoro Islands; which lie from Mozambique northwards. On the south side of the principal island is a very high land, so high that in a whole day's sail with a good wind we could not lose the sight thereof.

The same day, the ships separated themselves again, according to the ancient manner, for the occasions aforesaid.

The 3rd of September, we once again passed the Equinoctial line, and had sight of the North Star.

The 4th of September, we espied a ship of our own fleet, and spake with him. It was the *San Francisco*, which sailed with us till the 7th day, and then left us.

The 13th of September, we saw another ship, which was the *San Jago;* which sailed out of sight again and spake, not with us.

The 20th of September, we perceived many snakes swimming in the sea, being as great as eels: and other things like the scales of fish, which the Portuguese call *vintins* (which are Half Rials of silver, Portuguese money, because they are like unto it), which swim and drive upon the sea in great quantities; which is a certain sign and token of the Indian coast.

Not long after, with great joy we descried land, and found ground in forty-seven fathoms deep. It was the land of Bardes, which is the uttermost end and entry of the river of Goa; being about three miles from the city. It is a high land where the ships of India do anchor and unlade; and from thence their wares are carried by boats to the town. That day we anchored out in the sea, about three miles from the land; because it was calm and the flood tide was past: yet it is not without danger, and hath round about a fair and fast land to anchor in.

The 21st, being the next day, there came to us divers boats called *almadias* [*canoes*] which boarded us, bringing with them all manner of fresh victuals from the land, as fresh bread and fruit: Some of the boatmen were Indians that had been christened.

There came likewise a galley to fetch the Archbishop, and brought him to a place called Pangiin, which is in the middle way between Goa and the road of Bardes, and lieth upon the same river. Here he was welcomed and visited by the Viceroy of India, Don FRANCISCO MASCARENHAS, and by all the lords and gentry of the country, as well spiritual as temporal. The magistrates of the town desired him to stay there ten or twelve days, while preparation might be made to receive him with triumph into the city, as their manner is: which he granted them.

The same day, we entered the river into the road[stead] under the land of Bardes, being the 21st of September 1583, and five months and thirteen days after our putting forth of the river of Lisbon (including our stay of fifteen days at Mozambique): which was one of the speediest and shortest voyages that, in many years before and since that time, was ever performed. There we found the ship named *San Lorenzo* which arrived there a day before us.

The 22nd day, the *San Jago* came thither; and the next day after, arrived the *San Francisco*.

There died in our ship, thirty persons: among which some were slaves, and one a High Dutchman, that had been one of the King of Spain's Guard. Every man had been sick once or twice, and had let blood. This is ordinarily the number of men that die in the ships; sometimes more, sometimes less.

About ten or twelve years before, it chanced that a Viceroy for the King, named RUY LORENZO DETAVORA sailed for India, and had in his ship 1,100 men. There happened a sickness among them; so that there died thereof to the number of 900, who were all thrown overboard into the sea, before they came to Mozambique; the Viceroy himself being one. Which was an extraordinary sickness, and it is to be thought that the great number of the men in the ship was the cause of breeding the same. Therefore in these days the ships no longer take so many men with them: for with the number they do carry, they have stinking air and filth enough to cleanse within the ship.

The 30th of September, the Archbishop, my master, with

great triumph was brought into the town of Goa; and by the gentlemen and rulers of the country led into the Cathedral Church, singing *Te DEUM laudamus*; and after many ceremonies and ancient customs, they conveyed him to his palace, which is close by the Church.

The 20th of November, our admiral [*flag ship*] the *San Felipe* arrived at Cochin, without staying to land at any place; having endured much misery by the means before rehearsed, and having been seven months and twelve days under sail.

The last of the same month of November, the ships sailed from Goa to the coast of Malabar and Cochin, there to receive their lading of pepper and other spices. Some take in their lading on the coast of Malabar; and some at Cochin, which can always lade two ships with pepper. The ships unlade all their Portuguese commodities in Goa, where the merchants and factors are resident; and from thence sail along the coast to take in their lading. Each ship doth commonly lade 8,000 quintals of pepper, Portuguese weight. Every quintal is 128 [English] pounds. Then they come to Cochin, whither the Factors also do travel; and lade in cloves, cinnamon, and other Indian wares, as in my voyage homeward [*see pp.* 57-61, etc.], I will particularly declare.

In the months of January and February, *anno* 1584, the ships with their lading returned from Cochin, towards Portugal; with whom my brother went, because of his office in the ship: and I stayed with my master in India certain years to see and learn the manners and customs of the said lands, people, fruits, wares, and merchandise; with other things, which, when time serveth, I will in truth set down, as I for the most part have seen it with mine eyes.

JAN HUYGHEN VAN LINSCHOTEN.

Diary of occurrences in the Portuguese settlements in India, 1583–1588 A.D.

[*Discourse of Voyages &c.* 1598.]

Notice the marvellous security of the Portuguese in India at this time, under their triple protection: the Papal bull of 1494; the power of Spain; and England and Holland, as yet, quiescent and at home.

The exhaustive information which LINSCHOTEN gave of the East, led the way to the formation of the Dutch, and English East India Companies.

1583.

ABOUT the same time [*i.e., December* 1583], there came certain Jesuits to Goa, from the island of Japan; and with them, three Princes (being the children of Kings of that country) wholly apparelled like Jesuits: not one of them was above sixteen years of age. They were minded, by the persuasions of the Jesuits, to travel to Portugal; and from thence to Rome, to see the Pope: thereby to procure great profit, privileges, and liberties from him for the Jesuits; which was their only intent.

They continued in Goa till the year 1584, and then set sail for Portugal. From thence, they travelled into Spain: where, by the King and all the Spanish nobility, they were received with great honour: and presented with many gifts, which the Jesuits kept for themselves. Out of Spain, they went to see the Pope: from whom they obtained great privileges and liberties. That done, they travelled throughout Italy, as to Venice, Mantua, Florence; and all places and dominions in Italy: where they were presented with many rich presents, and much honoured; by means of the great report, the Jesuits made of them

To conclude. They returned again unto Madrid: where, with great honour, they took their leave of the King; with letters of commendation, in their behalf, unto the Viceroy and all the

Captains and Governors of India. So they went to Lisbon, and there took shipping, *anno* 1586, and came in the ship called *San Felipe* (which, on her return, was taken by Captain DRAKE); and after a long and troublesome voyage, arrived at Mozambique.

Where, the ship received her lading [homeward] out of another ship, called the *San Lorenzo* (ladened in India, and bound for Portugal), that, having lost her masts, had to put in there.

And, because the time was far spent to get into India, the said *San Felipe* took in the lading of the *San Lorenzo*; and was taken, in her way returning home, by the Englishmen: and was the first ship that was taken coming out of the East Indies; which the Portuguese took for an evil sign, because the ship bore the King's own name.

But returning to our matter. The Princes and the Jesuits of Japan, the next year after [*i.e.*, 1587], arrived at Goa, amidst great rejoicings and gladness; for that it was verily thought they had all been dead. When they came thither, they were all three apparelled in Cloth of Gold, and of Silver, after the Italian manner; which was the apparel that the Italian Princes and Noblemen had given them. They came thither very lively; and the Jesuits very proudly, for, by them, their voyage had been performed.

In Goa, they stayed till the monsoon or time of the winds came to sail for China; at which time, they went from thence, and so to China, and from thence to Japan; where, with great triumph and wondering of all the people, they were received and welcomed home, to the furtherance and credit of the Jesuits: as the book declareth, which they have written and set forth in the Spanish tongue, concerning their voyage, as well by water as by land, as also of the entertainment that they had in every place.

1584.

In the year 1584, in the month of June, there arrived in Goa many ambassadors, as from Persia, Cambaia, and from the *Samorin*, which is called, the Emperor of the Malabars, and also from the King of Cochin.

Among other things, there was a peace concluded by the Samorin and the Malabars with the Portuguese, upon condition that the Portuguese should have a fort upon a certain haven lying on the coast of Malabar, called Panane, ten miles from Calicut; which was presently begun to be built.

There, with great cost and charges, they raised and erected a fort; but because the ground is all sandy, they could make no sure foundation. For it sank continually, whereby they found it best to leave it; after they had spent in making and keeping thereof, at the least, four tons of gold, and reaped no profit thereof: intending thereby, if the Samorin should break his word, and come forth (as oftentimes he had done), that, by means of that haven, they would keep him in; where he should have no place to come abroad, to do them any more mischief. But seeing that the Malabars had many other havens and places, from whence they might put forth to work them mischief; and as much as ever they did (although the Samorin protested not to know of them; as also that he could not let [*hinder*] it, saying, "They were sea rovers, and were neither subject unto him, nor any man else"): they left their fort, and put no great trust in the Malabars, as being one of the most rebellious and traitorous nations in all the Indies; who make many a travelling merchant poor, by reason the sea coast is made by them, so dangerous and perilous to sail by.

For the which cause, the Portuguese army by sea [*i.e., their navy*] is yearly sent forth out of Goa, only to clear the coast of them: yet are there many Malabars, in divers places, who, by roving and stealing, do much mischief in the country, both by water and by land. They keep themselves on the seaside, where they have their creeks to come forth; and to carry their prizes in, to hide them in the country.

They dwell in straw houses upon stony hills, and rocks not inhabited, so that they cannot be overcome; neither do they care for the Samorin, nor any other man else.

There is a haven belonging to these rovers, about twelve miles distant from Goa, called Sanguisceu; where many of them dwell, and do so much mischief: that no man can pass by, but that they receive some wrong by them. So that there came, daily, complaints unto the Viceroy, who then was named Don FRANCISCO DE MASCHARENHAS, Earl of VILLA DORTA; who, to remedy the same, sent unto the Samorin, to will him to punish them: who returned the messenger again, with answer that "He had no power over them, neither yet could command them, as being subject to no man;" and gave the Viceroy free liberty to punish them at his pleasure, promising that he should have his aid therein.

Which the Viceroy understanding, prepared an army [*i.e., squadron*] of fifteen foists, over which he made chief Captain, his nephew, a gentleman called Don JULIANES MASCHARENHAS; giving him express commandment first to go unto the haven of Sanguisceu, and utterly to raze the same down to the ground.

This fleet being at sea, and coming to the said haven, the Admiral of the fleet asked counsel what was best to be done: because Sanguisceu is an island, lying with the coast, a river running about it, and many cliffs [*rocks*] and shallows in the entrance; so that, at low water, men can hardly enter in.

At the last, they appointed that the Admiral with half the fleet, should put in on the one side; and the Vice-Admiral, called JOAN BARRIGA, with the other half, should enter on the other side. Which being concluded, the Admiral, commanding the rest to follow, entered first, and rowed even to the firm land; thinking they were coming after: but the other Captains, who were all young and inexperienced gentlemen, began to quarrel among themselves, who should be first or last? whereby the fleet was separated. Some lay in one place, some in another, upon the banks and shallows, and could not stir; so that they could not come to help the Admiral, nor yet stir backwards or forwards. And when the Vice-Admiral should have put in on the other side; the Captains that were with him would not obey him, saying "He was no gentleman, and that they were his betters." Upon these, and such like points, most of the Portuguese enterprises do stand, and are taken in hand; whereby, most commonly, they receive the overthrow. By the same means, this fleet was likewise spoiled, and could not help themselves.

Which those of Sanguisceu, having forsaken their houses and being on the tops of the hills, seeing that the foists lay about, one separated from the other, upon the rocks and shallows, not able to put off; and that the Admiral lay alone upon the strand, and could not stir: they took courage, and, in great number, set upon the Admiral's foist; and put all to the sword, except such as saved themselves by swimming. And although the Admiral might well have saved himself, for a slave offered to bear him on his back; yet he would not, saying that "He had rather die honourably fighting against the enemy, than to save his life with dishonour." So that he defended himself most valiantly, but when so many came upon him that he could no longer resist them, they slew him; and cut off his head in presence of all the other foists. Which done, they stuck the head upon a pike, crying, in mocking, unto the other Portuguese, "Come and fetch your Captain again!" to their no little shame and dishonour, that in the meantime, looked one upon another, like owls.

In the end, they departed from thence with the fleet, every man severally by himself, like sheep without a shepherd; and so returned again to Goa with that great victory. The Captains were presently [*at once*] committed to prison, but, each man excusing himself, were all discharged again: great sorrow being made for the Admiral, especially by the Viceroy, because he was his brother's son; who was also much lamented by every man, as a man very well beloved for his courteous and gentle behaviour. The other Captains, on the contrary, were much blamed; as they well deserved.

Presently thereupon, they made ready another army, with other Captains, whereof Don JERONIMO MASCHARENHAS, who was cousin to the aforesaid one deceased, was Admiral, to revenge his death. This fleet set foot on land, and, with all their power, entered among the houses; but the Sangueseans that purposely watched for them, perceiving them to come, fled into the mountains, leaving their straw houses empty, whither they could not be followed by reason of the wildness of the place: whereupon the Portuguese burnt down their houses and cut down their trees, razing all things to the ground. With which destruction, they departed thence; no man resisting them.

At the same time, the [Portuguese] Rulers of Cochin began, by the commandment of the Viceroy, to set up a Custom House in the town; which till that time, had never been there. For which, the inhabitants rose up, and would have slain them that went about it. Whereupon they left off till such time as the new Viceroy, called Don DUARTE DE MENESES came out of Portugal; who, with the old Viceroy, assembled a Council at Cochin, where the Government was delivered unto him: where he used such means, that by fair words and entreaty, they erected their Custom House; and got the townsmen's goodwill, but more by compulsion than otherwise. Which custom is a great profit to the King, by means of the traffic therein used: for there the Portuguese ships do make themselves ready with their full lading, to sail from thence to Portugal.

The same year [1584], in the month of September, there arrived in Goa, a Portuguese ship, called the *Dom Jesus de Carania*, that brought news of four ships more that were on the way, with a new Viceroy called Don DUARTE DE MENESES: which caused great joy throughout the city, all the bells being rung, as the manner is, when the first ship of every Fleet arriveth in Goa, out of Portugal. In that ship came certain canoniers [*gunners*], Netherlanders; that brought me letters out of Holland, which was no small comfort to me.

Not long after, in the same month, there arrived another ship, called *Boa Viagen* [*p.* 38], wherein were many gentlemen, and Knights of the Cross that came to serve the King in India: among whom, was one of my Lord Archbishop's brethren, called ROQUE DA FONSECA [*p.* 37]. The other lords were Don JORGIE TUBAL DE MENESES, Chief Standard Bearer to the King of Portugal, newly chosen Captain of Soffala and Mozambique, in regard of certain service that he had, in times past, done for the King in India; JOAN GOMES DA SILVA, the new Captain of Ormus: and Don FRANCISCO MASCHARENHAS, brother of Don JULIANES MASCHARENHAS that was slain in Sanguisceu, as I said before, who was to have had the Captain's place of Ormus; but, by means of his death, it was given unto his brother Don FRANCISCO, for the term of three years, after he that is in it, had served his full time.

In November after, the other three ships arrived in Cochin. They had sailed outside of Saint Lawrence's Island [*Madagascar*], not putting into Mozambique. The ships' names were *Santa Maria*, *Arreliquias*; and the admiral [*flag ship*] *Las cinque chagas* or "The Five Wounds" [*i.e., of our Saviour, usually called, the Stigmata*]. In her, came the Viceroy Don DUARTE DE MENESES, that had been Captain of

Tangier in Barbary: and there were in this ship, nine hundred soldiers and gentlemen that came to safe conduct the Viceroy, besides above a hundred sailors. They had been above seven months upon the way, without taking [*touching*] land, before they arrived at Cochin: where the Viceroy was received with great solemnity.

Being landed, he presently sent to the old Viceroy, to certify him of his arrival; and that he should commit the Government of the country unto the Archbishop, to govern it in his absence (especially because the Archbishop and he were very good friends and old acquaintance; having been prisoners together in Barbary, when Don SEBASTIAN King of Portugal was slain): which the old Viceroy presently did, and went by sea to Cochin; that he might return to Portugal with the same ship, as the Viceroys use to do. For after their time of Government is out, they may not stay any longer in India.

The 10th of November, *anno* 1584, the ship called *Carania* went from Goa to Cochin; there to take in pepper and other wares. Then do all the Factors go to Cochin to lade their wares; and when the ships are laden and ready to depart, they return again to Goa: where they still remain. In that ship, the old Viceroy, with many gentlemen, sailed to Cochin.

1585.

The 5th of February 1585, the Viceroy, Don DUARTE DE MENESES, arrived in Goa; where he was received with great triumph and feasting.

In the month of April, the same year, my fellow, and servant to the Archbishop (called BARNARD BURCHERTS, and born in Hamburg [vol. I. *p.* 318]), travelled from Goa unto Ormus, and from thence, to Balsora; and from thence, by land, through Babylon, Jerusalem, Damascus, to Aleppo, from whence he sent me two letters, by an Armenian: wherein he certified me of all his voyage; which he performed with small charges and less danger, in good fellowship, and very merry in the company of the *Caffilas*. From Aleppo he went to Tripolis; and there he found certain ships for England, wherein he sailed to London; and from thence to Hamburg: which I understood by letters from him, written from thence.

In the month of August, there came letters from Venice

by land, that brought news of the murder of the Prince of ORANGE, a man of honourable memory; as also the death of the DUKE of ALENÇON or ANJOU; with the marriage of the Duke of SAVOY to the King of Spain's daughter.

The 20th of October, there arrived in Goa, the ship called the *San Francisco*, that came out of Portugal. In it, came some Dutch cannoneers, that brought me letters out of my country; with the news of the death of my father, HUYGHEN JOOSTEN of Harlem.

The 1st of November after [1585], arrived at Cochin, the *Sant Alberto* that came from Portugal. And the 1st of December, that year, there arrived at Cananor, upon the Malabar coast, the ship called the *San Lorenzo*; and from thence, came to Goa: most of her men being sick, and about ninety of them dead; they having endured great misery, and not having once put to land. At that time, there wanted [but] two of the Fleet that came from Lisbon in company with her: and they were the *San Salvador*, and the admiral [*flag ship*], *San Jago*; whereof they could hear no news.

At the same time, there arrived certain Italians, overland, in Goa, and brought news of the death of Pope GREGORY XIII., and of the election of the new Pope, called SIXTUS VI.

At that time, also, the ships that came from Portugal, sailed to Cochin, to take in their lading; which done, in the month of January 1586, they sailed for Portugal.

In the month of May 1586, letters were brought to the Viceroy and Archbishop at Goa, from the Captain of Soffala and Mozambique, to certify them of the casting away [*in the previous August*] of the admiral *San Jago*, that set out of Portugal, the year before, *anno* 1585.

She was cast away in this manner. The ship having come, with a good speedy wind and weather, from the Cape of Good Hope to Mozambique: they had passed, as they thought, all dangers; so that they needed not to fear anything. Yet it is good for the Master and others to be careful and keep good watch, and not to stand too much upon their own cunning and conceits, as these did; which was the principal cause of their casting away.

Between the Island of St. Lawrence and the firm land, in $22\frac{1}{2}°$ S., there are certain shallows [*shoals*] called the "India," ninety miles from the Mozambique. Those shallows are mostly of clear coral of black, white, and green colours, which is very dangerous. Therefore it is good reason they should shun them; and surely the Pilots ought to have great care, especially such as are in the Indian ships, because the whole ship and safety thereof lieth in their hands and is only ruled by them; and that, by express commandment from the King, so that no man may contrary them.

They being thus between the lands, and by all the sailors' judgements hard by the "Shoals of India" [*p.* 15], the Pilot took the height of the sun, and made his account that they were past the Shallows; commanding the Master to make all the sail he could, and freely to sail to Mozambique, without any let or stay. And although there were divers sailors in the ship, that likewise had their "cards," some to learn, others for their pleasure; as divers officers, the Master, and the Chief Boatswain, that said it was better to keep aloof, specially by night, and that it would be good to hold good watch because they found that they had not, as then, passed the Shallows: yet the Pilot said the contrary, and would needs show that he only had skill and power to command; as commonly the Portuguese, by pride, do cast themselves away; because they will follow no man's counsel, and be under no man's subjection, specially when they have authority. As it happened to this Pilot, that would hear no man speak, nor take any counsel but his own; and therefore commanded that they should do, as he appointed them.

Whereupon, they hoisted all their sails, and sailed in that sort till it was midnight, both with a good wind and fair weather; but the moon not shining, they fell full upon the Shallows, being of clear white coral, and so sharp that, with the force of wind and water that drave the ship upon them, it cut the ship in two pieces as if it had been sawn in sunder: so that the keel and two orlops [*i.e.*, *decks*] lay still upon the ground, and the upper part, being driven somewhat further, at the last, stuck fast; the mast being also broken.

Wherewith, you might have heard so great a cry that all the air did sound therewith: for that in the ship, being admiral [*flag ship*], there were at the least five hundred persons: among the which were thirty women, with many Jesuits and friars. So that, as then, there was nothing else to be done, but every man to shrift, bidding each other farewell, and asking of all men forgiveness; with weeping and crying, as it may well be thought.

The Admiral, called FERNANDO DE MENDOZA, the Master, the Pilot, and ten or twelve more, presently entered into the small boat, keeping it with naked rapiers, that no more should enter, saying they "would go and see if there were any dry place in the Shallows; whereon they might work to make a boat of the pieces of the broken ship, therein to sail unto the shore, and so to save their lives." Wherewith, they put them that were behind in some small comfort; but not much. But when they had rowed about, and finding no dry place, they durst not return again unto the ship: lest the boat should have been overladen and so drowned; and in the ship, they looked for no help. Wherefore, in fine, they concluded to row to land; having about twelve boxes of marmalade, with a pipe of wine and some biscuit, which, in haste, they had thrown into the boat; which they dealt among them, as need required. So commending themselves to GOD, they rowed forwards towards the coast; and after they had been seventeen days upon the sea, with great hunger, thirst, and labour, they fell on the land: where they saved themselves.

The rest that stayed in the ship, seeing the boat came not again; it may well be thought what case they were in. At the last, one side of the upper part of the ship, between both the upper orlops, where the great boat lay, burst out; and the boat being half burst, began to come forth: but, because there was small hope to be had, and few of them had little will to prove masteries, no man laid hand thereon, but every man sate looking one upon another. At the last, an Italian, called CYPRIAN GRIMOALDO, rose up, and taking courage unto him, said, "Why are we thus abashed? Let us seek to help ourselves, and see if there be any remedy to save our lives!" Wherewith presently, he leaped into the boat, with an instrument in his hand, and began to make it clean; whereat some others began to take courage, and to help him as well as they could, with such things as first came to their hands. So that in the end, there leaped, at the least, fourscore and ten persons into it, and many hung by the hands upon the boat swimming after it, among the which were some women: but because they would not sink the boat, they were forced to cut off the fingers, hands, and arms of such as held thereon, and let them fall into the sea; and they threw many overboard, being such as had not wherewith to defend themselves.

Which done, they set forward, committing themselves to GOD; with the greatest cry and pitifullest noise that ever was heard, as though heaven and earth had gone together: when they took their leave of such as stayed in the ship. In which manner, having rowed certain days, and having but small store of victuals; for that they were so many in the boat that it was ready to sink, it being likewise very leaky and not able to hold out. In the end, they agreed among themselves to chose a captain, to whom they would obey and do as he commanded: and among the rest, they chose a gentleman, a *Mestizo* [*half-caste*] of India; and swore to obey him. He presently commanded to throw some of them overboard, such as, at that time, had least means or strength to help themselves. Among the which, there was a carpenter that had, not long before, helped to dress the boat: who seeing that the lot fell upon him, desired them to give him a piece of marmalade and a cup of wine; which when they had done, he willingly suffered himself to be thrown overboard in the sea, and so was drowned.

There was another of those, that in Portugal are called New Christians. He being allotted to be cast overboard in the sea, had a younger brother in the same boat, that suddenly rose up and desired the Captain that he would pardon and make free his brother, and let him supply his place, saying, "My brother is older, and of better knowledge in the world than I, and therefore more fit to live in the world, and to help my sisters and friends in their need: so that I had rather die for him, then to live without him." At which request, they let the elder brother loose, and threw the younger at his own request into the sea; who swam at the least six hours after the boat. And although they held up their hands with naked rapiers willing him that he should not once come to touch the boat: yet laying hold thereon, and having his hand half cut in two, he would not let go; so that in the end, they were constrained to take him in again. Both the which brethren, I knew, and have been in company with them.

In this misery and pain, they were twenty days at sea; and in the end got to land: where they found the Admiral and those that were in the other boat.

Such as stayed in the ship, some took boards, deals, and other pieces of wood; and bound them together, which the Portuguese call *Jangadas* [*rafts*]; every man what they could catch, all hoping to save their lives: but of all those, there came but two men safe to shore.

They that had before landed out of the boats, having escaped that danger, fell into another; for they had no sooner set foot on shore, but they were spoiled by the inhabitants of that country, called Kaffirs, of all their clothes: whereby they endured great hunger and misery, with many other mischiefs, which it would be over tedious to rehearse. In the end, they came unto a place where they found a Factor of the Captains of Soffala and Mozambique, and he helped them as he might; and made means to send them unto Mozambique: and from thence, they went into India; where I knew many of them, and have often spoken with them.

Of those that were come safe to shore, some of them died before they got to Mozambique. So that in all, there were about sixty persons that saved themselves. All the rest were drowned or smothered in the ship; and there was never other news of the ship than as you have heard.

Hereby, you may consider the pride of this Pilot; who, because he would be counselled by no man, cast away that ship with so many men: wherefore a Pilot ought not to have so great authority, that, in time of need, he should reject and not hear the counsel of such as are most skilful.

This Pilot, when he came into Portugal, was committed to prison; but, by gifts and presents, he was let loose: and another ship [*San Thomas*], being the best of the Fleet that went for India, *anno* 1588, was committed unto him; not without great curses and evil words of the mothers, sisters, wives, and children of those that perished in the ship, which all cried "Vengeance on him!"

And coming with the ship, called the *San Thomas*, wherein he then was placed, he had almost laid her on the same place, where the other was cast away; but day coming on, they room themselves off [*gave it a wide berth*], and so escaped.

Yet in their voyage homeward to Portugal, the same ship was cast away by the Cape of Good Hope [*pp.* 70, 78], with the Pilot and all her men: whereby much speech arose, saying "It was a just judgement of GOD against him, for making so many widows and fatherless children."

This I thought good to set down at large, because men might see that many a ship is cast away by the headiness of the Governors, and the unskilfulness of the Pilots: wherefore it were good to examine the persons before a ship be committed unto them; especially a ship of such a charge, and wherein consisteth the welfare or undoing of so many men, together with their lives; and impoverishing of so many a poor wife and child.

This loss happened in the month of August, *anno* 1585.

1586.

In May, *anno* 1586, two ships, laden with ware, set sail out of the haven of Chaul in India, that belonged unto certain Portuguese inhabitants of Chaul; the owners being in them. Those ships should have sailed to the Straits of Mecca or the Red Sea, where the said merchants used to traffic; but they were taken by two Turkish galleys that had been made in the innermost parts of the Red Sea, in a town called Suez. The said galleys began to do great mischief; and put all the Indian merchants in great fear.

The same month, there was a great army prepared in Goa, both of foists and galleys, such as had not been seen in many years; and was appointed to sail to the Red Sea, to drive the Turkish galleys away, or else fight with them if they could. They were also commanded by the Viceroy to winter their ships in Ormus: and then to enter into the Straits of Persia [*Persian Gulf*], lying behind Ormus; and to offer their services to XATAMAS [*ABBAS I.*], King [*Shah*] of Persia, against the Turk, their common enemy. Thereby to trouble him on all sides, if they had brought their purpose to effect; but it fell out otherwise, as you shall hear.

For Chief of this army, there was appointed a gentleman named RUY GONSALVES DA CAMARA, who had once been Captain of Ormus; being a very fat and gross man, which was one of the chief occasions of their evil fortune. With him, went the principal soldiers and gentlemen of all India; thinking to win great honour thereby.

This army being ready, and minding to sail to the Red

Sea; they found many calms upon the way, so that they endured much misery, and began to die like dogs, as well for want of drink as other necessaries. For they had not made their account to stay so long upon the way; which is always their excuse, if anything falleth out contrary to their minds. This was their good beginning, and as it is thought a preparative to further mischief. For coming to the Red Sea, at the mouth thereof, they met the Turkish galleys; where they had a long fight: but, in the end, the Portuguese had the overthrow; and escaped, as well as they might, with great dishonour and no little loss.

The Turks being victorious, sailed to the coast of Melinde, where they took certain towns, as Pate and Brava, that, then, were in league with the Portuguese: there to strengthen themselves, and thereby to reap a greater benefit, by damaging the Portuguese, and lying under their noses.

The Portuguese army having sped in this manner, went to Ormus, to winter themselves there; and, in the meantime, to repair their army, and to heal their sick soldiers, whereof they had many.

When the time served to fulfil the Viceroy's commandment, in helping XATAMAS, having repaired their foists; the General, by reason of his fatness and corpulent body, stayed in Ormus: and appointed as Lieutenant in his place, one called PEDRO HOMEN PEREIRA (who, although he was but a mean gentleman, yet was he a very good soldier, and of great experience): commanding them to obey him in all things, as if he were there in person himself.

He gave them also in charge to land, as they sailed along the coast of Arabia, to punish certain pirates that held a place called Nicolu [? *Nackiloo*]; and spoiled such as passed to and fro upon the seas; doing great hurt to the ships and merchants of Bussorah that trafficed to Ormus: whereby the traffic to the said town of Ormus was much hindered, to the great loss and undoing of many a merchant.

With this commission, they set forward with their Lieutenant; and being come to Nicolu; they ran their foists on shore, so that they lay half dry upon the sand. Every man in general leaped on land, without any order of battle; as in all their actions they use to do: which the Lieutenant perceiving, would have used his authority, and have placed them in order as is requisite to be done in warlike affairs. But they, on the contrary, would not obey him, saying, "He was but a boor! and that they were better gentleman and soldiers than he!" With these, and such like presumptuous speeches, they went on their course; scattering here and there in all disorder, like sheep without a shepherd: thinking all the world not sufficient to contain them, and every Portuguese to be a HERCULES, and so strong that they could bear the whole world upon their shoulders.

Which the Arabs, being within the land and mostly on horseback, perceiving (and seeing their great disorder; and knowing most of the foists to lie dry on the strand, and that, without great pain and much labour, they could not hastily set them afloat), presently compassed them about, and being ringed in manner of a half moon, they fell upon them; and, in that sort, drave them away, killing them as they listed, till they came unto their foists: and because they could not presently [*at once*] get their foists into the water, they were compelled, through fear and shame, to fight; where likewise many of them were slain, and not above fifty of them escaped that had set foot on land. So having got into their foists, they rowed away.

In this overthrow, there were slain about eight hundred Portuguese, of the oldest and best soldiers in all India. Among them was a trumpeter, being a Netherlander; who, being in the thickest of the fight, not far from the Portuguese Ensign, and seeing the Ensign-bearer throw down his Ensign (the easier to escape and save his life), and that one of the Arabs had taken it up: casting his trumpet at his back, he ran with great fury, and with his rapier killed the Arab that held it, and brought it again among the Portuguese, saying, "It was a great shame for them to suffer it to be carried away." In that manner, he held it, at the least, a whole hour, and spoiled many of the Arabs that sought to take it from him, in such manner, that he stood compassed about with dead men: and although he might have saved himself if he would have left the Ensign, yet he would not do it; till, in the end, there came so many upon him that they killed him, where he yielded up the ghost with the Ensign in his arms. And so ended his days with honour; which the Portuguese themselves did confess, and often acknowledged it; commending his valour: which I thought good to set down in this place, for a perpetual memory of his valiant mind.

The Lieutenant, perceiving their disorder and how it would fall out, wisely saved himself, and got into the foists, where he beheld the overthrow; and in the end, with empty vessels, he turned again to Ormus, without doing anything else: to the great grief and shame of all the Indian soldiers; being the greatest overthrow that ever the Portuguese had in those countries, or wherein they lost so many Portuguese together. Among the which, was the Archbishop's brother [*p.* 27], and many other young and lusty gentlemen, of the principal [families] in all Portugal.

At the same time [*i.e., in the spring of* 1587], the Queen of Ormus came to Goa, being of MAHOMET's religion, as all her ancestors had been before her; and as then, contributory [*subject*] to the Portuguese. She caused herself to be christened, and was brought, with great solemnity, unto the town; where the Viceroy was her godfather, and named her Donna PHILLIPPA, after the King of Spain's name: being a fair white woman, very tall and comely. With her, likewise, a brother of hers, being very young: and, then, with one MATTHIAS D'ALBUQUERQUE, that had been Captain of Ormus, she sailed to Portugal [*in the* Nostra Señora da Sancao; *see pp.* 40-51; *which arrived in Portugal on* 12*th of August* 1587, *see p.* 51] to present herself to the King.

She had [*or rather,* afterwards] married with a Portuguese gentleman, called ANTONIO DAZEVEDO COUTINHO; to whom, the King, in regard of his marriage, gave the Captainship of Ormus, which is worth [*in the three years*] about 200,000 ducats [= *about* £50,000 *then* = £300,000 *now*].

[The following occurrence must have been after LINSCHOTEN's departure from India, in November 1588.]

This gentleman, after he had been married to the Queen about half a year, living very friendly and lovingly with her, he caused a ship to be made, therewith to sail to Ormus; to take order there for the rents and revenues belonging to the Queen, his wife. But his departure was so grievous unto her, that she desired him to take her with him; saying that "she could not live without him!" but, because he thought it not then convenient, he desired her to be content; promising to return again with all the speed he might. Whereupon, he went to Bardes, which is the uttermost part of the river entering into Goa, about three miles off. While he continued there, staying for wind and weather; the Queen, as it is said, took so great grief for his departure, that she died the same day that her husband set sail and put to sea: to the great admiration [*wonder*] of all the country; and no less sorrow, because she was the first Queen, in those countries, that had been christened, forsaking her kingdom and high Estate, rather to die a Christian, and be married to a mean [*private*] gentleman than to live like a Queen under law of MAHOMET. And so was buried with great honour, according to her estate.

In the month of August 1586, there arrived a man of Mozambique in Goa, that came from Portugal in the ship that should sail to Malacca [*usually leaving Lisbon about February: in this instance, about February* 1585] that brought news unto the Viceroy, how the ship, called the *Boa Viagen*, that, in the year before [*i.e., January* 1585 *see p.* 27], sailed from India towards Portugal, was cast away by the Cape of Good Hope: where it burst in pieces, being overladen (for they do commonly overlade most of their ships), and affirmed that the ship had, at the least, nine handsful height of water within it, before it departed from Cochin; although, before their ships set sail, they put the Master and other Officers to their oaths, thereby to make them confess "If the ship be strong and sufficient to perform the voyage, or to let them know the faults!" Which, upon their said oaths, is certified by a *Protestation*, whereunto the Officers set their hands. Yet, though the ship have so many faults, they will never confess them, because they will not lose their places and the profit of the voyage; yea, although they do assuredly know the ship is not able to continue the voyage: for covetousness, overthrowing wisdom and policy, maketh them reject all fear; but when they fall into danger, then they can speak fair, and promise many things.

In that sort, most of the ships depart from Cochin, so that if any of them come safely to Portugal, it is only by the will of GOD; for, otherwise, it were impossible to escape, because they overlade them, and the ships are, otherwise, so badly provided, and with little order among their men: so that not one ship cometh home but can show of their great dangers by overlading, want of necessaries, and reparations of the ship, together with unskilful sailors; yet for all these daily and continual dangers, there is no amendment, but they daily grow worse and worse.

In this ship, called the *Boa Viagen*, were many gentlemen of the best and principal, that had served a long time in India; travelling then into Portugal, with their certificates, to get some reward for their service, as the manner is. Because it was one of the best and greatest ships of that fleet, the Ambassador of XATAMAS [*ABBAS I.*], King [*Shah*] of Persia, went therein, to procure a league with the King of Spain, to join with him against the Turk, their common enemy: but he being drowned, the Persian would send no more Ambassadors; and yet he is still in league and good friendship with the Portuguese.

The worst ship that saileth from Cochin to Portugal, is worth, at the least, a million of gold [*i.e., of ducats = about £300,000 then=about £1,800,000 now*], and this was one of the best ships; whereby it may be considered what great loss cometh by the casting away of one of their ships, besides the men. For there never passeth a year; but one or two of they are cast away, either in going or coming.

In the month of September, the same year, 1586; there arrived four ships out of Portugal, in Goa, called the *San Thomas*, *San Salvador* [*p.* 44], the *Arreliquias*, the *Dom Jesus de Carania*: but of their admiral, the *San Felipe*, they had no news since their departure from Lisbon.

On the last of November, the same ships departed from Goa: some along the coast of Malabar, to take in their lading of pepper, and from thence to Cochin; others direct to Cochin, where commonly one or two of them are laden with pepper, and where, alone, all other kind of wares are laden.

At the same time, there was a ship called the *Ascention*, that lay in Goa, and had made certain voyages to China and Japan: which ship was bought by the Factors for Pepper, because the ship *Carania*, by reason of her oldness, was broken in Cochin, and set upon the stocks there, to be new made; but was not finished, by reason of a certain controversy that fell among the Factors.

In this ship, [newly] called *Nostra Señora da Sancao*, my Lord the Archbishop sailed to Portugal, by reason of certain quarrels newly begun between the Viceroy with other Councillors, and the Archbishop. And although he was entreated by the Viceroy, all the Council, gentlemen and communalty of Goa, not to leave them; yet he would not be dissuaded from his purpose, but went to ride unto the King, of whom he was well beloved: which the Viceroy and others liked not very well, fearing he should give some information to the King, which would be smally to their profit.

In that mind, he undertook his voyage, discharging all his servants; saving some that he kept about him for his service: and leaving no man in his house, but only his Steward and myself, to receive his rents, and keep his house. And because, as then, the Golden Jubilee or Pardon of Rome, called *La Santa Crusada*, was newly brought into the Indies (being granted to the end that, with the money that should be gathered by virtue thereof, the Captains and prisoners in Africa or Barbary, that had been taken prisoners in the battle wherein Don SEBASTIAN, King of Portugal, was slain, should be redeemed); the Golden Jubilee was sent unto the Archbishop: who, being appointed the Roman Apostolic Commissary, &c., for the same, made me the General Clerk throughout all India, to keep account of the said receipts; and gave me one of the keys of the chest wherein the money lay, with a good stipend, and other profits belonging to the same, during the time of his absence. Thereby the rather to bind me, that I should remain in his house, and keep the same till his return again; as I had promised unto him.

1587.

So he set sail from Cochin, in the month of January, *anno* 1587; his Pilot being the same man that cast the *San Jago* away upon the "Flats of India," as it is said before [*pp.* 30-33].

The ships, at that time, being ready to set sail, one some four or five days after the other, as they were laden (for they observe a certain order therein, the better to register all their wares and merchandise), it so fell out that all the other ships being despatched; the *Arrcliquias* only was the last that laded. Which ship having taken in her whole lading, the

Officers, and some of the Factors, being bribed, suffered some of the ballast to be taken out, and in place thereof laded cinnamon: for, at that time, cinnamon was risen, and at a very high price in Portugal; and therefore the Officers and Factors, by gifts aforesaid, suffered it to be laden in that manner, having no other place to lade it in.

You must understand that when the time cometh to set sail, the ships lying at anchor about a mile within the sea, where they received their lading (the reason why they lie so far is because it is summer time; and there the sea is as calm and still, as if it were within the land), a trumpet is sounded throughout all the town of Cochin to call them all on board: wherewith, all that will sail, do presently come down, accompanied with their friends, which, in small boats called *Tones* and *Pallenges*, bring them aboard; with great store of bread, and such like victuals. So that you shall, many times, see the ships hung round about with boats, at the least three or four hundred; with such a noise and rejoicing, as it is wonderful to hear.

Sometimes the ships are so ladened that the cables touch the water, and besides that, the hatches are covered with divers chests, seven or eight one above another; they having no other place to set them in: for that under the hatches they are so stuffed, that there is not any empty room. So that when they set sail, they know not where to begin, nor how to rule the ship; neither can they well, for a month after, tell how to place all things in order.

So it was with this ship, which being thus prepared, the *Viador da Fazenda*, or the King's Officers, came aboard, asking "If the ship were ready to set sail, and depart?" They say, "It was ready." And he having made a *Protestation* or Certificate thereof, the Officers set to their hands, as some say; but others deny it. Presently he commanded them to wind up their cables and hoisted anchor, as the manner is. So they let their sails fall, with a great cry of *Boa Viagen!* "GOD send them good fortune, and a merry voyage!" all the boats being still aboard [*attached*]; which commonly do hang at her at least a mile or half a mile within the sea; because it is calm.

This ship, called the *Arreliquias*, beginning in this manner to sail, among other romage [*lumber*] that stood on the hatches, there were certain hens' cages; from whence, certain hens flew out: whereupon every man claimed them for his own, and, upon a Sunday, as in such cases it is commonly seen, they ran all on a heap upon one side; whereby the ship (being light of ballast, and laden with many chests above the hatches, as I said before) swayed so much on the one side that, by little and little, it sank clean under the water, so that not above a handful of the mast could be seen above the water.

The people leaped into the boats that, as yet, were hanging above the ship, which was good fortune for them; otherwise, there had not one escaped alive: but, by that means, they were all saved; excepting only the slaves, that were bound with iron chains and could not stir, and so were drowned.

GOD knoweth what riches were lost in her! For nothing was saved, but some few chests that stood above the hatches; which the duckers [*divers*] got up, and yet the goods in them were, in a manner, spoiled: the rest was utterly lost.

By this, it may be considered what manner the Portuguese use in lading of their ships; and that it is to be thought that the many ships that are cast away, whereof there hath been heard no news or tidings, are only lost by means of evil order and government.

This being so unluckily fallen out, the Merchants used all the speed and means they could, by witnesses, to make Protestation against the Officers and Factors of the pepper, that they might be punished for taking out the ballast: but they kept themselves out of the way; and, by prolonging of time, it was forgotten, and nothing done therein. So the Merchants, that had received all the loss, were glad to put it up.

In the same month [*January* 1587], came news out of Malacca, that it was in great danger, and that many died there for hunger; as also that the ship that went from Portugal thither, was forced to stay there, because they had no victuals to despatch it away [*pp.* 43, 46]: and likewise, that the Strait of Sumatra was kept by the enemy, so that there no ships could pass that way to China or Japan. This was done by the kings [*chiefs*] of Sumatra, that is to say, the kings of Achen [*Achin*] and Jor, lying by Malacca upon the firm land; who rebelled against the Portuguese in Malacca, upon a certain injury done unto them by the Captain there.

This news put Goa in a great alteration, for their principal traffic is to Malacca, China, and Japan, and the islands bordering on the same: which, by reason of these wars, was wholly hindered. Whereupon a great number of foists, galleys, and ships were prepared in Goa to relieve Malacca, and all the townsmen tasked [*taxed*], every one at a certain sum of money, besides the money that was brought from other places; and men taken up to serve in ships, for by means of their late overthrows, [the Portuguese] India was, at that time, very weak of men.

In the month of May, *anno* 1587, there came a ship or galley of Mozambique unto Goa, brings news that the ship, the *San Felipe*, had been there, and taken in the lading of pepper that was in the ship called the *San Lorenzo* [*p.* 29] that had arrived there in her voyage towards Portugal, and was all open above the hatches and without masts, most of her goods being thrown into the sea: whereby, miraculously, they saved their lives, and, by fortune, put into Mozambique. In this ship, called the *San Felipe*, were the young princes, the Kings' children of Japan, as is before declared [*at p.* 22-3].

The same galley which brought this news from Mozambique to Goa, likewise brought news of the army that sailed out of Goa, in December 1586, being the year before, unto the coast of Melinde, to revenge the injury which they had received in the fleet whereof RUY GONSALVES DA CAMARA was Captain, as I said before; as also to punish the towns that, at the same time, had united themselves with the Turk, and broken league with the Portuguese [*p.* 34-7]. Of this army was General, a gentleman called MARTIN ALONZO DE MELLO.

Wherewith, coming upon the coast of Abex or Melinde, which lyeth between Mozambique and the Red Sea, they went on land; and, because the Turks whom they sought for, were gone home through the Red Sea, they determined to punish and plague the towns that favoured the Turks, and broken their alliance with them. To this end, they entered into the country as far as the towns of Pate and Brava, that little thought of them, and easily overran them; for the most part of the people fled to save themselves, and left their towns. Whereby the Portuguese did what pleased them, burning the towns with others that lay about them, and razing them to the ground: and among those that fled, they took the King [*chief*] of Pate, whose head, in great fury, they caused to be stricken off, and brought it to Goa; where, for certain days, it stood on a mast in the middle of the town, for an example to all others, as also in sign of victory.

Wherewith, the Portuguese began to be somewhat encouraged. So they went from thence to Ormus; and from Ormus they were to go to help the King of Persia, as the Viceroy had commanded them. But being at Ormus, many of their men fell sick and died: among the which the General, MARTIN ALFONSO DE MELLO was one. Whereupon they returned unto Goa; without doing any other thing.

The same army sailing to the coast of Abex, and falling on the island of Zanzibar (which lieth 6° S. about seventy miles from Pate towards Mozambique, about eighteen miles from the firm land), they found there the *San Salvador* [*p.* 39] that came from Cochin, sailing towards Portugal: which was all open, having thrown all her goods overboard, saving only some pepper which they could not come at; and was in great danger, holding themselves, by force of pumping, above the water. They were upon the point to leave, being all weary and ready to sink: which they certainly had done, if, by great good fortune, they had not met with the army; which they little thought to find in those parts.

The army took the ship with them to Ormus, where the rest of the pepper and goods remaining in her were unladen, and the ship broken in pieces: and of the boards, they made a lesser ship, wherein the men that were in the great ship, with the rest of the goods that were saved in her, sailed to Portugal: and, after a long and wearisome voyage [*p.* 82], arrived there in safety.

The 17th of September, 1587, a galliot of Mozambique arrived at Goa, bringing news of the arrival of four ships in Mozambique, that came out of Portugal. Their names were the *Sant Antonio, Sant Francisco, Nostra Señora da Nazareth,* and the *Sant Alberto*: but of the *Santa Maria* that came in company with them from Portugal, they had no news. Afterwards they heard, that she put back again to Portugal, by reason of some defaults in her, and of the foul weather.

Eight days after [*25th of September*], the said four ships arrived in Goa, where they were received with great joy.

At the same time, the fort called Colombo, which the Portuguese hold in the island of Ceylon, was besieged by the King of Ceylon, called Raju [? *Rajah*] and in great danger of being lost: to deliver which, there was an army of foists and galleys sent from Goa; whereof BERNARDINE DE CARVALHO was General.

And at the same time, departed another army of many ships, foists, and galleys, with a great number of soldiers, munition, victuals, and other warlike provisions; wherewith to deliver Malacca: which as then was besieged and in great misery, as I said before. The General thereof was Don PAULO DE LIMA PEREIRA, a valiant gentleman, who, not long before, had been Captain of Chaul; and being very fortunate in all his enterprises, was therefore chosen to be General of that fleet.

The last of November, the four ships aforesaid, departed from Goa; to lade at Cochin, and from thence to sail to Portugal.

The December after, while the fort of Colombo, in the island of Ceylon, was still besieged; the town of Goa made out another great fleet of ships and galleys: for the which they took up many men within the city, and compelled them to go in the ships, because they wanted men; with a great contribution of money raised upon the merchants and other inhabitants, to furnish the same. Of which army was appointed General, MANUEL DE SOUSA COUTINHO, a brave gentleman and soldier, who, in times past, had been Captain of the said fort of Colombo, and had withstood a former besieging: whereupon the King put him in great credit, and advanced him much; and, after the Viceroy's death, he was Viceroy of [Portuguese] India, as in time and place we shall declare [*p.* 50].

He arrived, with his army, in the isle of Ceylon, where he joined with the other army that went before; and placed themselves in order to give battle to RAGIU: who, perceiving the great number of his enemies, brake up his siege, and forsook the fort, to the great rejoicing of the Portuguese. Having strengthened the fort with men and victuals, they returned again to Goa; where, in the month of March, *anno* 1588, they were received with great joy.

In the month of April, the same year [1588], the army of

DON PAULO DE LIMA PEREIRA that went to Malacca, arrived in Goa with victory: having freed Malacca, and opened the passage again to China and other places.

The manner whereof was thus. In their way, as they passed the Straits of Malacca, they met with a ship belonging to the King of Achen [*Achin*] in Sumatra; who was a deadly enemy to the Portuguese, and the principal cause of the besieging of Malacca.

In the same ship was the daughter of the said King of Achen; which he sent to be married to the King of Jor, thereby to make a new alliance with him against the Portuguese: and, for a present, he also sent him a goodly piece of ordnance, whereof the like was not to be found in all India. Therefore it was, afterwards, sent to Portugal as a present to the King of Spain, in a ship of Malacca; which, after, was cast away in the island of Terceira, one of the Flemish Isles [*Azores, see pp.* 97-101]: where the same piece, with much labour, was weighed up, and laid within the fortress of the same isle; because it is so heavy that it can hardly be carried into Portugal.

But to the matter. They took the ship with the King's daughter, and made it all good prize. By it, they were advertised what had passed between the Kings of Achen and Jor: so that presently [*at once*] they sent certain soldiers on land, and marching in order of battle, they set upon the town of Jor, that was sconced [*pallisadoed*] and compassed about with wooden stakes, most of the houses being of straw. Which, when the people of the town perceived, and saw the great number of men, and also their resolution, they were in great fear; and, as many as could, fled, and saved themselves in the country.

To conclude. The Portuguese entered the town and set it on fire, utterly spoiling and destroying it, razing it even with the ground, slaying all they found; but taking some prisoners, whom they led away captives. They found within the town, at the least, 2,500 brass pieces, great and small, which were all brought into India [*i.e., Goa*]. You must understand that some of them were no greater than muskets; some greater; and some very great, being very cunningly wrought with figures and flowers, which the Italians and Portuguese that have denied [*renounced*] their faith, and become Mahometists have taught them: whereof there are many in India, and are those indeed that do most hurt. When they have done any murder or other villany; fearing to be punished for the same, to save their lives, they run over by the firm land among the heathens and Moors: and there they have great stipends and wages of the Indian kings and captains of the land.

Seven or eight years before my coming into India [*i.e.*, 1575 *or* 1576], there were in Goa, certain Trumpeters and Cannoneers, being Dutchmen and Netherlanders; and because they were rejected and scorned by the Portuguese in India (as they scorn all other nations in the world); as also because they could get no pay; and when they asked for it, they were presently abused and cast into the galleys, and there compelled to serve: in the end, they took counsel together, and seeing they could not get out of the country, they secretly got unto the firm [*main*] land of Balagate and went unto Hildalcan [? *the Deccan*]; where they were gladly received, and very well entertained with great pay, living like Lords. And there, being in despair, denied [*renounced*] their faith; although it is thought by some, that they remain still in their own religion: but it is most sure that they are married there, in those countries, with heathen women; and were living when I came from thence.

By this means are the Portuguese the cause of their own mischief, only through their pride and hardiness; and make rods to scourge themselves withal: which I have only showed in respect to those cast pieces and other martial weapons, which the Indians have learnt of the Portuguese and Christians; whereof in times past, they had no understanding. And although they [of Jor] had placed all those pieces in very good order; yet it should seem they knew not how to shoot them off or to use them as they should: as it appeared hereby, for that they presently forsook them, and left them for the Portuguese.

With this victory, the Portuguese were very proud; and, with great glory, entered into Malacca: wherein they were received with great triumph: as it may well be thought, being delivered by them from great misery wherein they had long continued. Which the King of Achen hearing, and that his daughter was taken prisoner, he sent his Ambassador to

Don PAULO DE LIMA PEREIRA, with great presents, desiring to make peace with him: which was presently granted, and all the ways to Malacca were opened, and all kinds of merchandise and victuals brought thither, which before had been kept from them; whereat was much rejoicing.

This done, and order being taken for all things in Malacca; they returned again to Goa: where they arrived in safety (as I said before) in the month of April [1588]; and there, were received with great triumph; the people singing *Te DEUM laudamus*; and many of the soldiers bringing good prizes with them.

In the month of May [1588] following, upon the 15th of the same month, the Viceroy Don DUARTE DE MENESES died in Goa; having been sick but four days, of a burning fever, which is the common sickness of India, and is very dangerous: but it is thought it was for grief, because he had received letters from the Captain of Ormus, wherein he was advertised that they had received news, over land, from Venice, that the Archbishop was safely arrived at Lisbon, and well received by the King; and because they were not friends at his departure (as I said before), they said, "He was so much grieved thereat, that fearing to fall into the displeasure of the King, by information from the Bishop, he died of grief."

But that was contrary [to the facts] as, hereafter, by the ships, we understood; for the Bishop died in the ship [*on the 4th August* 1587], eight days before it arrived in Portugal. So they kept company together; for they lived not long one after the other, whereby their quarrel was ended with their lives.

The Viceroy's funerals were observed, with great solemnity, in this manner.

The place appointed for the Viceroys' burial is a Cloister called *Reis Magos* or "The Three Kings of Cologne," being of the Order of Saint Francis, which standeth in the land of Bardes, at the mouth of the river of Goa.

Thither was his body conveyed, being sent in the Royal Galley, all hanged over with black pennons, and covered with black cloth; and accompanied with all the nobility and gentlemen of the country.

Approaching near the Cloister of *Reis Magos*, being three

miles from Goa down the river towards the sea; the friars came out to receive him, and brought his body into the church, where they placed it upon a hearse; and so, with great solemnity, sang *Mass*.

Which done, there were certain letters, called *Vias*, brought forth; which are always sealed, and, by the King's appointment, kept by the Jesuits: and are never opened, but in the absence or at the death of the Viceroy.

These *Vias* are sent yearly by the King, and are marked with the figures 1, 2, 3, 4, 5, and so forth. When there wanteth a Viceroy, then the first number or *Via* is opened; wherein is written, that in the absence or after the death of the Viceroy, such a man shall be Viceroy. If the man that is named in the first *Via* be not there; then they open the second *Via*, and look whose name is therein; being in place, he is presently [*immediately*] received and obeyed as Governor. If he be likewise absent; they open the rest, orderly, as they are numbered, until the Governor be found: which, being known, they need open no more. The rest of the *Vias* that are remaining are presently shut up, and kept in the cloister of the Jesuits: but before the *Vias* are opened, there is no man that knoweth who it shall be, or whose name is written therein.

These *Vias* are opened, with great solemnity, by the Jesuits, and read in open audience, before all the nobles, Captains, Governors, and others that are present. If the man that is named in the *Vias*, be in any place of India or the East countries, as Soffala, Mozambique, Ormus, Malacca, or any other place of those countries, as sometimes it happeneth; he is presently sent for: and must leave all other offices, to receive that place, until the King sendeth another out of Portugal. But if the man named in the *Vias* be in Portugal, China, or Japan, or the Cape of Good Hope; then, they open other *Vias*, as I said before.

The *Mass* being finished, the Jesuits came with the King's packets of *Vias*, which are sealed with the King's own signet, and are always opened before the other Viceroy's body is laid in the earth. And there, they opened the first *Via*, and, with great devotion, staying to know who it should be; at the last, was named for Viceroy, one MATTHIAS D'ALBUQUERQUE, that had been Captain of Ormus, and, the year before [*i.e.*,

January 1587, *see* vol. i. *pp.* 312, 325; vol. ii. *p.* 37], had gone, in company with the Archbishop, to Portugal, because he had broken one of his legs, thinking to heal it: but if he had known as much, he would have stayed in India. [*He was appointed Viceroy in* 1590, *see pp.* 114-5].

He, being absent, the second *Via* was opened, with the like solemnity, and herein they found named for Viceroy, MANUEL DE SOUSA COUTINHO (of whom I made mention before, [*p.* 45] and who was the man that raised the siege in the island of Ceylon), to the great admiration [*wonderment*] of every man: because he was but a mean [*poor*] gentleman; yet very well esteemed, as he had well deserved by his long service.

Although there were many rich gentlemen in that place, whom they thought rather should have been preferred thereto: yet they must content themselves, and show no dislike. Thereupon they presently saluted him kissing his hand, and honoured him as Viceroy.

Presently, they left the dead body of the old Viceroy, and departed in the galley, with the new Viceroy; taking away all the mourning cloths and standards, and covering it with others of divers colours and silks.

And so entered into Goa, sounding both shalms and trumpets; wherein he was received with great triumph, and led to the great Church, where they sang *Te DEUM laudamus*, &c., and there gave him his oath to hold and observe all privileges and customs, according to the order in that case provided.

From thence, they led him to the Viceroy's Palace, which was presently all unfurnished by the dead Viceroy's servants; and furnished again by the new Viceroy, as the manner is, in all such changes and alterations.

The body of the dead Viceroy being left in the Church, was buried by his servants, without any more memory of him; saving only touching his own particular affairs.

In the months of June, July, and August of the same year, *anno* 1588, there happened the greatest winter that had, of long time, been seen in those countries. Although it raineth every winter, never holding up, all the winter long; but not in such quantity and abundance as it did in those three months, for it rained continually and in so great abundance, from the 10th of June till the 1st of September, that it could not be judged that it ever held up from raining, one half hour together, either night or day; whereby many houses, by reason of the great moisture, fell down to the ground; as also because the stone wherewith they are built is very soft, and the greater part of their mortar is more than half earth.

The 16th of September 1588, there arrived in Goa, a ship of Portugal, called the *San Thomas*, bringing news of four ships that were in Mozambique, all come from Portugal: which, not long after, came likewise to Goa. Their names were *San Christopher*, being admiral; *Santa Maria*, *Sant Antonio*, and *Nostra Señora de Consepcao*.

By these ships, we received news of the death of my Lord the Archbishop, Don Frey VINCENTE DA FONSECA, who died in his voyage to Portugal, upon the 4th day of August, *anno* 1587, between the Flemish Isles [*Azores*] and Portugal; eight days before the ship came to land.

It was thought that he died of some poison that he brought [in himself] out of India, or else of some impostume that suddenly brake within him. For an hour before his death, he seemed to be as well as ever he was in all his life: and suddenly he was taken so sick that he had not the leisure to make his will, but died presently: and voided at the least a quart of poison out of his body.

To be short. He was clothed in his Bishop's apparel, with his mitre on his head, and rings upon his fingers, and put into a coffin: and so thrown into the sea.

[illegible] month of [illegible] of September, that it could not [illegible] that [illegible] from [illegible] together [illegible] [illegible] abroad the [illegible] wheresoever [illegible] there [illegible] of them [illegible]

[illegible] of September [illegible] [illegible] ships that [illegible] of [illegible] all come from Portugal which [illegible] of Goa. Their names were [illegible] being admiral [illegible] and [illegible]

By these ships we received news of England [illegible] [illegible] the voyage [illegible] upon the [illegible] day of August [illegible] [illegible] land.

It was thought that [illegible] of India, or else [illegible] that [illegible] [illegible] and [illegible] and did [illegible] and [illegible] of the [illegible]

[illegible] into [illegible]

JAN HUYGHEN VAN LINSCHOTEN.

Return Voyage from Goa to Enkhuisen.

1588-1592 A.D.

THIS news [*i.e., of the death of his master, the Archbishop of the Indies; on the 4th of August* 1587, *which reached Goa in September* 1588, *see p.* 51] made many sorrowful hearts in India of such as were his well-willers and friends: and, to the contrary, such as hated him were glad and rejoiced; because he had been earnest to reprehend and correct them for their faults. But none lost more by it than we, that were his servants, who looked for great preferment by him; as without doubt he meant to have obtained it of the King, as being one of the principal occasions of his going into Portugal: but death altered all.

And although, at that time, my meaning and intent was to stay the coming [back] of my Lord Archbishop; and to continue longer there, yea, possibly, while I lived: yet, upon this news, I was wholly altered in my purpose; and a horrible fear came upon me, when I called to mind what I had passed, touching the things I was desirous to bring to pass. And although I had means enough there, to get my living in good sort; being, as it were, one of those countrymen, and so, in all places well esteemed and accounted of: yet those persuasions were not of force enough, once to dissuade me from the pretence and desire I had to see my native country. So that it seemed, my GOD had opened mine eyes; and, by my Lord's death, made me more clear of sight, and to call my native soil unto remembrance: which, before, was so darkened that I had almost forgotten it; and stood in hazard never to see it any more, if my Lord had lived, and returned home again [to Goa].

But to avoid all occasions and inconveniences that might happen, and daily offered themselves to me, I resolutely determined to depart: whereunto I sought all the means and necessary occasions I could find, to bring it to pass. And that which persuaded me most thereunto, was the loss of my brother, WILLIAM TIN, that had been with me in India [*pp.* 2, 7]: who, sailing from Setubal, in Portugal, towards Hamburg, taking his course on the back side of England [*i.e., round Ireland and Scotland*], was cast away; and neither ship nor men could ever be heard of.

Being in this resolution, it chanced that a ship, by authority of the Viceroy, and at the request of the Farmers of Pepper, was appointed to sail for Portugal; because there was so great a quantity of pepper to be laden, that the Portuguese ships [*i.e., the Fleet of Carracks*], at that time, could not take it in. Although the ships are purposely sent to lade pepper, with licence from the King, that there may no more but five ships lade every year; whereunto, the Factors do bind themselves: yet if there be any goods in India, as pepper and other wares, which these ships cannot take in; then the Farmers of Pepper and the King's Officers may buy one or two ships, and make them ready for the purpose to take it in, so that the ships be found that be sufficient. Which if the Factors refuse, then the Viceroy and the King's Officers may freight as many ships as they think good, and as they find fit to take it in; and lade them with the Farmers' pepper or any other goods that are there to be laden: so it be after the five ships are laden by the Farmers. And all this, for the profit of the King, without let or hindrance of the said Farmers.

In this sort, as I said before, there was a ship, called the *Santa Cruz*, that was built in Cochin by the King of the Malabars (and called after the name of the town of *Cochin*, that was likewise, by the Portuguese, called *Santa Cruz*), which the King of the Malabars made in honour of the Portuguese, because he hath brotherly alliance with them, and is called "Our Brother in arms" by the King of Portugal.

The same ship, being of 1,600 tons, he had sold to a Portuguese, that therewith had made a voyage into China and Japan; and because it was strong and good, and so, fit to make a voyage to Portugal; and because (as I said before) there was more pepper than the Portuguese ships could take in: the Farmers of Pepper were desirous to buy it, and besought the Viceroy to let them have it; according to the contents of their composition [*contract*] and the King's Ordinance.

Whereupon, the Viceroy caused the Farmers of the Ships to be called together, and signified unto them what the request of the Farmers of Pepper was, that is to say, that the ship should be bought, according to the King's Ordinance, forasmuch as necessity did so require it, and they had refused to use it, saying that "it was not fit for them": and so desired, in respect of the King's interest in the pepper, the ship might be bought accordingly; always provided, that the King's Ordinance, who granted them their Privilege, might be kept and observed, viz., that their ships might first have their lading, and be first despatched.

And although they that had bought it of the owners, for 10,000 ducats [=£2,660 13*s*. 4*d*. *then* = *about* £16,000 *now*] ready money, were in doubt that they should find wares enough to lade it withal: yet, in the end, it was, in a manner, laden as well as the other ships were.

Now it was agreed by the owners that sold it, that the Master Gunner and Chief Boatswain should keep their places still within the ship; as they had, when it sailed to China and Japan. The Gunner's name was DERICK GARRITSON, of Enkhuisen; who, after he had been twenty years in India, was minded, as then, to sail in that ship for Portugal: with whom, because of old acquaintance and for his company, I minded to see if I could get any place within the ship.

And because the Farmers of Pepper had their Factors in India, that were Dutchmen; which lay there in the behalf of the Foukers and Velsares of Augsburg; who, at that time, had a part of the pepper laden in that ship, and use to send in each ship a Factor, to whom the King alloweth a cabin and victuals for the voyage: this place of Factor in the said ship called the *Santa Cruz*, I did obtain of the Farmers; because they were of my acquaintance.

Whereupon I prepared myself to depart, and got a passport of the Viceroy (without which no man may pass out of India); and also a certificate out of the King's Chamber of Accounts, and out of the *Matricola General*; wherein all such as come into India are registered, with a note of my pay, which, by the King's commandment, is appointed to be paid upon certificate from thence; and withal the time of my residence in India and what place I was employed in there: that when I came to Portugal, I might have recompense if I would ask it, or [could go back, if I] minded to return again into India.

But, although I had no such intent; yet must I, of force, observe this order, to make them think that I would return again, and the easier to obtain my passport: which was easily granted me by the Governor, as also the other certificates.

Having obtained them, I took my leave of all my friends and acquaintance, not without great grief: as he that was to depart out of his second natural dwelling-place, by reason of the great and long continuance I had made in those countries; so that I was, in a manner, half dissuaded from my pretended voyage. But, in the end, the remembrance and affection of my true natural country got the upper hand, and overruled me; making me wholly to forget my conceit unto the contrary: and so, committing myself and my affairs unto GOD (who only can direct and help us, and give good success to all endeavours), I entered into my new pretended course.

In the month of November, 1588, the ships sailed again from Goa, to the coast of Malabar and Cochin to take in their lading.

And the 23rd of the same month, the *Santa Cruz* set sail; to begin our voyage.

The 28th day, we arrived at Honor [*Honawur*], a fort belonging to the Portuguese, and the first they have upon the coast of Malabar. It lieth southward from Goa, eighteen miles. In which place, we were assigned to take in our lading of pepper.

They used not, before, to lade any pepper in that place; so that we were the first that ever laded there; but from henceforward they minded, yearly, to lade one ship there. For the Queen of Batticola, that lays not far from thence, and Honor, which is within her jurisdiction or kingdom, had bound herself to deliver, yearly, 7,000 or 8,000 Quintals [= *about* 1,000,000 *English lbs.*] of pepper; so that the Farmers paid her half the money for the same, six months before she delivered it; and then she would deliver it at times [*by instalments*]. For the which cause, the owners have their Factor at Honor, to receive it of her, by weight; and to lay it up till the time of lading cometh.

The like have they in all the other forts upon the coast of Malabar, as at Mangalore, Barselor, Cananor, Cochin, Coulan [*Quilon*], &c.

The Farming of the Pepper; and, also, of the Carracks that bring it to Portugal.

NOw to know the right manner of Farming of the Pepper, you must understand,

That the Farmers take the same to farm for five years, and bind themselves to send every year their stock of ready money [*i.e., about* 260,000 *Pieces of Eight, at* 436 *Reis* (= 69·76*d.*) *each* = *about* £75,000 *then* = *about* £450,000 *now*], for 30,000 Quintals of pepper; so that the King will send ships to lade it in. The King, on the other side, bindeth himself to perform, and to send, every year, five ships, the Farmers bearing the adventure [*risk*] of the sea, both of their money sending thither, and of the pepper brought from thence; and must lade it, in India, into the ships, at their own costs and charges. Which being brought to Portugal, they deliver up the pepper to the King, at the price of 12 ducats the Quintal [*i.e.*, £3 4*s. the Quintal of* 128 *lbs.*; *or Sixpence the lb. then=Three Shillings now*]: and if any be cast away or taken upon the sea, it is at the Farmers' charge; for the King dealeth only but with that which is delivered to him in Portugal, being dry and fair, lade up in the King's Storehouse in Lisbon. For the which, he payeth not any money unto the Farmers until the said pepper be sold; with the money whereof he payeth them.

So that the King; without any hazard or disbursing anything of his own, hath always his money for his pepper; without the loss of any one penny.

And in respect of that, the Farmers have great and strong privileges. First, that no man, of what estate or condition soever he be, either Portuguese or of any place in India, may deal or trade in pepper but they, upon pain of death: which is very sharply looked unto. Likewise, they may not, for any occasion or necessity whatsoever, diminish or lessen the ordinary stock of money [*i.e., the* 260,000 *Reals of Eight*], neither hinder nor let them, in any sort, concerning the lading thereof: which is also very strictly observed. For, although the pepper were for the King's own person, yet must the Farmers' pepper be first laden: to whom, the Viceroy and other Officers and Captains of India must give all assistance, help, and favour, with watching the same, and all other things; whatsoever shall be required by the said Farmers, for the safety and benefit of the said pepper.

For the lading and providing whereof, the said Farmers are to send their Factors, servants, and assistants, of what nation soever they be (except Englishmen, Frenchmen, and Spaniards), unto every place, to see it ladened and despatched away. For other strangers may not go to India; without the special licence of the King or of his Council for India.

The pepper commonly costeth in India 28 Pagodas the Bhar. Every Bhar is 3½ Portuguese Quintals. So that every Quintal standeth them in 12 Pardaos Xeraphines and 4 Tangas [*see* vol. i. *p.* 320]:

(Every Quintal is 128 [English] pounds; and every Pardao is 3 Testons or 30 Stivers, heavy money: and every Tanga is 60 Reis or 6 Stivers),

Which is 12 Dollars (of 60 Pence Flemish the piece) after the rate of the Portuguese money, and 24 Stivers of the like money: besides all charges, and adventure of the sea. But the great quantity making them gain the more, especially if it come safe home.

[By equivalent values of the coins, at *p.* 320 of vol. i., the *Pagoda* was then equal to 76·8*d.* We may therefore represent the statement in the text thus.

English lbs.		*Quintal.*	*Bhar.*			£	*s.*	*d.*	
				@	8 Pagodas, the *Quintal* =	2	11	2	4¾*d.* the English
128	=	1			*or its equivalent, viz.,*				lb. then = *about*
448	=	3½	= 1		28 Pagodas, the *Bhar* =	8	19	1	2*s.* 4½*d. now.*

As the Pepper was sold to the King at Sixpence the English lb. for which the Farmers paid 4¾*d.*, their outside profit would be about 30 per cent. on an invested capital in pepper alone of about £75,000 then [=£450,000 *now*]. From which, vast deductions should be made, for peculations, losses, &c. : which were, no doubt, partially compensated for, by the Farmers robbing the King as well as they could. So that it was thievery from beginning to end.

The Farmers also brought home many other things than pepper, such as cinnamon, spices, fancy ware; on which, no doubt, there was a vast profit.

It is clear from this arrangement, that when the English took Portuguese Carracks, it was not King PHILIP II. who was the first sufferer; but the Speculators, both of the Ships, and their Cargoes; who might be of many countries, as of Augsburg, *p* 55.

It is interesting to trace the rise in the price of these Eastern commodities, in their progress to the consumer. The wholesale English price of the pepper captured by the Earl of CUMBERLAND's fleet on the 13th July 1589, was estimated at Two Shillings [=12*s. now*] the English lb. : see *p.* 187 of vol. ii. The King's profits thereon must therefore have been enormous.]

The ships and their freighting, with conditions to build them and the provision of all necessaries for them, are also farmed by themselves: and all, at the adventure of the Farmers [of the Carracks]. If the ship come safe home, they give the King a certain sum of money for every ship; and every year furnish five ships, likewise at their own charges: but such soldiers as are appointed to go in them, are bound to sail for the King; and have only meat and drink at the Farmers' charges. The officers and sailors are placed therein, by the King's Admiralty: which the Farmers may not once deny or refuse.

So that the King adventureth nothing, neither in pepper nor in ships: but only if the ships be cast away he loseth the money that he should have had for the Farm of every ship, if it had returned safe; and the Gain of the pepper, that should have been delivered him at a certain price.

Whereupon the Admiralty of Portugal are now waxen very careless to see them well conveyed, as they used to be during the times of the Kings of Portugal; when all the pepper came for the King's own account.

And although the King hath promised continually to send his Navy by sea as far as the Flemish Islands [*Azores*]; there to stay for the coming of the Indian ships, and from thence to convey them to Lisbon: yet since they were farmed out, there are few fleets sent forth; so that they are but little thought upon. But howsoever it is; in the payment of the Fee Farm for pepper, the King will not lose a penny of his due, nor once abate them anything.

Shipping the pepper in the Carracks.

THE 6th of December, we had taken in our lading of pepper, which was 6,700 Quintals [=*about* 380 *English tons*] of the best that is in all Malabar; and were very full.

The same day, we set sail from thence, keeping close under the coast: because that ordinarily in that country, every day, from twelve o'clock of the night till twelve at noon, there bloweth an Easterly wind, which cometh out of the land; and then cometh a West wind out of the sea, to the landward. With these two winds, we [here] perform our voyage. But the East wind is always mightier and stronger than the West, and therefore the ships keep themselves close under the shore: for when they put further in the sea, they can hardly get at the coast again; because the West wind is not of so great force. As it chanced unto us, for having put somewhat from the coast; we had much to do before we could get to the coast again: by which means, oftentimes, they lose their voyage to Portugal, as by experience it hath been found.

All the coast of Malabar is very pleasant to behold, for they sail so close to it, that a man may tell every hill, valley, and tree that is therein; being a very green and fair land.

The 11th of December, we came to Cananor, another fortress of the Portuguese. There we lay a day and a half, to take in certain masts, with other provisions that we were to use; which are there in great abundance.

So we set sail again, keeping along the coast, and passed by Calicut, Panane, and certain other places, until the 24th of December, when we arrived at Cochin: where we lay till the 20th of January, *anno* 1589.

In the meantime, our ship was provided of all things necessary; and then we stayed, till our turn came to set sail:

because the other ships, according to the contract, were to set sail before us, one after another. Which custom, I will here partly set down in brief.

You shall understand that as soon as the ship hath taken in her lading of pepper; which is done with great care and diligent watch, as well in the King's behalf as of the Farmers'; and is laden on the two nether orlops, that is, upon the ballast, and in the orlop next over it: laying deal boards upon the ballast, and making certain places and divisions for the purpose, with a hole over each place to shut in the pepper; and leaving room by the mainmast to pass by it. So that there are, at the least, thirty several places, which they call *payoos*; and all in the two lower orlops, as I said before: which, being all filled with pepper, they shut the holes of those places very close with oakum and pitch; and so they are marked with numbers, how many they are, and upon each place its weight of pepper.

These two orlops, being thus laden, there is left a place about the mainmast to bestow water, wine, wood; and other necessaries for the ship, which are daily used.

In the third orlop, and, on both sides thereof, there are divers places severally made, that belong to the Officers of the ship, as the Captain, Master, Pilot, Factor, Purser, &c.; and of all the rest of the sailors that are allowed places: which they sell or let out unto the Merchants to lade goods therein; whereof they make good profit. Upon the same orlop, from the mast to the stern, are the places where they put their powder, biscuit, sails, cloths, and other provisions for the ship.

The other orlops above these, are laden by the merchants with all sorts of wares; which are in chests, fats, balls, and packs; and are placed in this sort, that is to say,

As soon as the pepper is laden, there are presently sent into the ship two Waiters, and one that stoweth the goods, as a Porter; on the King's behalf. He hath ten or twelve porters under him that only must lade and stow the goods in the ship: the Master, nor any other, not once, having anything to do with it; saving only the Chief Boatswain, who is to look unto it, and yet commandeth nothing.

No goods may be laden whatsoever or how small soever they be, but they must be registered in the King's books; and they must bring a billet [*invoice*] from the *Veador da*

Fasenda, that is to say, the "Surveyor of the business," being Chief Officer for the King: wherein must be certified every kind of ware, by piecemeal, which they lade; together with the name of the ship wherein it is to be laden. For without that certificate, the Stowers and Porters will not take it in; and, although you have your billet, yet must you bribe the Waiters, before you can get it aboard the ship: and something must be given likewise to the Porters, besides their duties, if you desire to stow your goods well, otherwise they will let it stand. And he that giveth most hath the best place in the ship. Yea, and they stow the ship so miserably full, that there is not a hole or an empty place to be found, but it is full stuffed: and all for their profit. It is oftentimes seen, that the Chief Porter, that doth only command and look over the rest, getteth for his part, in bribes, for stowage of a ship, sometimes 700 or 800 ducats [=£190 *to* £215 *then=about* £1,100 *to* £1,300 *now*], and the Waiters as much; and this only by gifts.

These offices are given by favour of the Viceroy, and the *Veador de Fasenda*: which is the cause that the ships are oftentimes laden so full that they are in a manner ready to sink; so that a man would think it were impossible for them, either to row or stir. Because the Officers and sailors of the ships have nothing to do therewith, until the last hour that it setteth sail, and then it is delivered into their hands; and the Waiters and Porters go their ways, leaving the ships full in every place, even to the uppermost orlop: where there standeth commonly seven or eight chests, one above the other, both in the stern and foreship, upon the cables, in the forecastle, in the stirrige [*steerage*] and in every place, which are all full of great pots, fats, chests, hens' cages, and such like; so that it seemeth rather a Labyrinth or a Maze than a ship.

So they commit themselves to the grace of GOD, and set sail: and oftentimes it falleth out, as it did in our ship, that of fifty sailors which are above the ship, not above ten of them could tell how to steer, or to handle the rudder: and besides that, most of them were never at sea before, but get their places by favour as all the rest do; so that, being at sea, when occasion serveth, they stand looking one upon another, doing nothing, but cry, *Misericordia!* and, "Our Lady! help us!"

In Cochin, there are a great number of boats called *Tones*

that are cut out of one piece of wood; and yet, some of them are so great that a man may lade twenty pipes of water in them. These they carry aboard the ships, that lie at least a mile within the sea, and there they make price with them for a small sum of money; and then they go and fill the pipes themselves, with pots which they have for the purpose: and it is a great commodity to them. This water is brought out of the river of Cochin, called Mangate, and it is very good.

Cochin to Saint Helena.

AND now I will show unto you the manner that is used in the ships, when they sail home again: which, in part, I have already touched; as also of our departure and voyage from India to Lisbon.

1589.

The 1st January 1589 [*N.S.*], the *Santa Maria* set sail; and because it was one of the oldest ships, it was first despatched away; by reason that the sooner they depart from Cochin, they come in better time to the Cape of Good Hope: and the later they come thither, the more storms and foul weather they have, because as then the sun goeth further into the north and leaveth the south parts. Therefore commonly they let the best and strongest ships go last; because they are best able to hold out: and they stay the one for the other in the island of Saint Helena, until the 25th day of May, and no longer, which is the time appointed by the King; and so go, in company together, to Portugal. For from India unto the island of Saint Helena they need not keep company; because all that way they fear no rovers: and to that island, they have all their cannon shot pulled in [? *guns run in*], the better to pass the foul weather at the Cape of Good Hope.

The 6th of January, the ship, called *Nostra Señora de Consepcao* set sail.

The 10th of the same, the admiral [*flag ship*], called *San Christopher*.

The 12th, the *Sant Antonio*.

The 15th, the *San Thomas*, which was the greatest and best ship in all the fleet; and the richest of lading.

And the 20th of the same month, we set sail in our ship, called the *Santa Cruz*, being the last: wherein were about 200 men of all sorts; as sailors, soldiers, and slaves.

For from India there go but few soldiers, without the Viceroy's passport; by virtue thereof they go to present their services, and to fetch their pays and duties for the same. And this they do, after they have served in India some years; and also when they have ability to pass over: for when they are poor, and have no help, they must stay in India; even for necessity's sake, because they have no means to procure their passage. So that many of them are constrained to tarry there, and to marry Moors and Indian women, the better to maintain themselves; although it be with misery enough. For the charges of a man's voyage out of India is, at the least, 200 or 300 Pardaos (=£40 *to* £60 *then*=£240 *to* £360 *now*), and that only for meat and drink; which a poor soldier can hardly compass, unless he can procure some gentleman, Captain, or wealthy man in office to be favourable unto him, in helping him to perform his journey.

For in the voyages homeward, the King giveth nothing to each of the soldiers and passengers, but a free passage for himself and a chest of four spans high and broad, and seven spans in length; and that, after they have been three years in India. For that chest, they pay neither freight nor custom. They have likewise a chest in the roomage [*hold*] free of freight, for which they pay custom; and this they may sell to any merchant, as they commonly do, and is worth unto them, at the least, 40 or 50 Pardaos [=£10 *to* £12 10s. *then* =£60 *or* £75 *now*]. These places they call "Liberties," and he that buyeth them registereth them in the name of him that he buyeth them of; to the end, that in Portugal, they may enjoy the same liberty and privilege.

All the sailors and Officers of the ships, that sail in them from Portugal, have likewise, besides their places in the ships, the forage of such a chest allowed them, free of custom and freight.

All these things are very sharply looked into. For although the ships and goods are farmed; yet when they arrive at Lisbon, all the chests are brought into the Indian House, and there visited [*searched*], to see if any goods be in them that are forbidden to be brought out of India, as pepper, anill [*cochineal*], or indigo, and other such wares as are farmed of the King, and, if any be found, it is presently forfeited: and all the wares that are in such chests are likewise valued; so that if they amount to more than the value of 1,000 Milreis [=£666 13*s*. 4*d*. *then*=£4,000 *now*], they must pay custom for the over plus: which, in the time of the Kings of Portugal, was not used. For then, they were accustomed to carry their chests home, and to show them only to the Waiters: and although the poor sailors and Officers do much complain for the loss and breaking of their "liberties"; yet can they not be heard.

Thus there come but few soldiers out of India, for the causes aforesaid. For I certainly believe that of the 1,500 soldiers and more, that, yearly, are sent thither out of Portugal; there returneth not a 100 again. Some dying there in the country, others being cast away, and slain by divers occasions: and the rest, by poverty, not able to return again, and so, against their wills, are forced to stay in the country. If any of them do chance to come [back], it is with some Viceroy, Captain, or other gentleman, or person that hath borne office or authority. And when such men come over [to Portugal], they always bring some soldiers with them, to whom they give meat and drink; and yet, are such as are of their acquaintance, and that had been long before at their commandment: which they do, for the most part, upon a certain pride and vain glory.

And, in this sort, there may, yearly, come 20 or 30 soldiers over, in each ship, which have their slaves and Blacke Mores with them; so that they come clean and sweet home, both for linen and other things. Because linen is very good cheap in India: and the ships, when they return home, are cleaner than when they set out of Portugal; as they have fewer men in them, and such as come out of India bring all their necessaries with them. Besides, the ship is very sweet, by reason of the spice with that is laden in it.

The partition of the ship is in this manner.

The Pilot hath his cabin above in the hinder part of the ship, on the right side, where he hath two or three rooms;

and never cometh under [the] hatches, nor down into the foreship: but standeth only, and commandeth the Master of the ship to hoist or let fall the sails; and to look unto his course, how they shall steer; to take the height of the sun; and every day, to write and mark what passeth, how they sail, and with what tokens, wind, and weather.

The Master hath his cabins in the same place, behind the Pilot's cabins, on the left hand; with as many places and rooms as the Pilot hath: where he standeth, and commandeth with a silver whistle, and looketh only to the main mast and her sails; and so backwards [*i.e., all masts and rigging astern of it*]: yet he hath the care of all the ship and whatsoever belongeth to it; and commandeth all things, as to make and mend the sails, which he cutteth out and the sailors sew them. He looketh also if there be any fault in the ship, and causeth it to be mended: and, as need requireth, to draw their cannon in, and again to put it out.

If he wanteth anything, as cloth for sails, nails, ropes, or any such like things, as are needful; he must have them of the Factor and Purser of the ship; which presently are delivered unto him, with a note, of his hand[writing] in the book, to be accountable for it.

The Chief Boatswain hath his cabin in the Forecastle [*i.e., the Castle in the front part of the Carrack, rising in three short decks above the main deck in the centre of the ship*]; and hath commandment and government over the Fouke mast [*Foremast*] and the fore sails. He hath also a silver whistle, like the Master; and taketh care for all things belonging to the Fouke mast, and for the fast binding of the anchors.

The Guardian or Quartermaster hath his cabin close by the great mast outward on the left hand; for on the right hand, standeth the scullery and kitchen, where they dress their meat. He weareth a silver whistle, and hath charge to see the swabers pump, to make the ship clean; to look to the ropes, and cause them to be mended; and to the boat, which he commonly ruleth.

The Gunner hath his cabin inward from the mast, hard by the rudder, under the first orlop: and must always sit by the main mast, looking upon the Master, both night and day; that, as the Master whistleth to will the gunners to draw in their pieces or to thrust them out, he may be ready so to do.

He likewise taketh care for the pieces, and the things belonging to them; when they have cause to use them.

The Under Pilot doth nothing, but help the Chief Pilot, and watch his quarter. They have likewise two or three of the best sailors, that do nothing else but command in the Pilot's room, when he sleepeth.

The sailors have most of their cabins in the forecastle and thereabouts: and the gunners behind, by the Master Gunner, under the upper deck; and do nothing else but, with their instruments [*implements*], put the great pieces forth or draw them in, as they are commanded.

The Swabers must do all whatsoever they are bidden to do by the Officers, but never touch the rudder. For the sailors do only steer and rule the ship when need requireth, but not the pump. Neither do they hoist up the main sail: for the soldiers and slaves use to do that. The swabers pump.

The Carpenter doth such work as is to be done. The Cooper, in like sort: and also the Caulker. So that if the ship were sinking, not any of them will do more than belongeth to his charge: and what is further to be done, they will stand still, and look upon it.

The Captain hath the Gallery, and the cabin behind. He commandeth only over the soldiers, and such as watch by night.

The Pilot, Master, and the Chief Boatswain, are served in very good sort, with their silver lamps, beakers [*goblets*], cups, and bowls; every [*each*] man by himself: and are waited on by their slaves and servants, and have enough of everything. But the other sailors and swabers have not such store, but endure more hardness: for every man must provide for himself, as we told you before.

Now you must understand that in their ships, there is no Average. For when there happeneth any loss, or that any goods are thrown overboard; he standeth to the loss that oweth [*owneth*] the goods, without any more accounts: and that commonly falleth out upon the poor swabers, for they usually have their chests standing upon the hatches; because they have nothing to give unto the Porters that they might have a good place for them, as others, of greater ability use to do. And when any storm or hurt chanceth; then they throw the things overboard that first come to hand: without respect of persons, or any average to be made.

In this sort, setting sail; we held our course south-south-east for the space of 150 miles till we came to 7° S. of the Equinoctial line [*Equator*]; and from thence south-west-by-west unto the Cape of Good Hope: which way was never used before that time.

For they used to sail from Cochin south-west; and south-west-by-south between the Maldive islands, and a thousand other islands and sands [*shoals*] unto the island of St. Lawrence [*Madagascar*]; and so to the Cape. But after that the Pilot had lost the *San Jago* [in 1586] upon the "Shallows of India" [*pp.* 30-3], and escaped alive (he was now Pilot of the *San Thomas*, the best ship in all our fleet); he had, the fore voyage [*the preceding one to this, in* 1587] kept aloof 200 or 300 miles out into the sea, clean from all islands, sands, or cliffs: saying that "the casting away of so many ships, whereof no news or tidings could ever be heard, was that they were cast away upon the sands [*shoals*]; even as it chanced unto him," and to avoid the dangers thereof, as also to win the favour of the King and the Officers of the Admiralty, he was the first that took upon him to discover that way, with the ship wherein my Lord the Archbishop sailed [*p.* 40]. It is almost the same way, that the ships that came from Malacca do hold, when they sail to Portugal; wherein they see neither islands nor sands, nor any other thing, but only the plain sea.

So he came unto Portugal, certifying the Admiralty of that new way; and although he was cast into prison for the same cause, yet, by favour, he was presently released: and the Admiralty (perceiving it to be so great a danger for the ships to sail among the islands and sands, which they thought to be the chief cause of the loss of so many ships) have expressly commanded that the Pilots should use that new discovered way, according to the said Pilot's information, thereby to avoid all danger.

But that is not the cause of their casting away; although many times, they are the means of much mischief: but the chief reasons are, the unreasonable lading and charging of the ships, the unskilful seamen, and the slack visiting or searching of the ships, to see if they be fit to sail and have all things that they want. By these, and such like means, the ships are daily lost, as in other places [*pp.* 32, 34, 62,] by examples, and true witnesses, I have already declared; and as the same

Pilot, that first found the New Way, did well approve and verify to be true in the *San Thomas*, that the sands or islands did him no hurt, but only the overlading of her: wherewith, the ship was burst in pieces, by the Cape; as hereafter I will show [*pp.* 78, 82]. Notwithstanding, this way is not therefore to be disliked, although it be somewhat further about; but it is a very good way, and wholly out of all danger of sands and islands.

The 30th of January, in the night, we passed the Equinoctial line; and the next day, after, we descried a ship, which we thought to be the *San Thomas.*

The same day, one of our boys fell overboard; to save whom, we made all the haste we could to get out our small boat: but because it stood full of things, we could not so soon get it forth, but that in the meantime, the boy was cast at the least two miles behind us; and so was drowned.

The 3rd of February, the ship we saw, came close by us, and then we knew it to be the *San Thomas.* We made towards it to speak with them; but when they began to know our ship by the ropes, which were all white, being made of Indian *cairo* (fibre), and knowing that we were left behind them at Cochin (for they had thought when they had descried us, we had been one of the ships that first set sail) as also that their ship was accounted one of the best for sailing in all the fleet: for very pride and high stomach, they would not stay to speak with us; but made from us again. Which our Officers perceiving, did likewise wind from them; every [*each*] one doing his best to get before the other.

By this, and such like signs of pride, the Portuguese do often cast themselves away; and, as it may be conjectured, it was one of the chief causes of the loss of the *San Thomas*: for that they used all the means they could, to sail well, and that they might pass the Cape before us; whereof they use [*are accustomed*] to brag, when they meet at the island of Saint Helena; as if it were done by their wisdom.

So it fell out with the *San Thomas*, that coming to the Cape of Good Hope, it had a contrary wind, whereby they struck all their sails, and so lay driving against the waves of the sea, which do fall against a ship as if it struck against a hill: so that if the ship were of hard stones, yet, in the end, they would break in pieces; much more such ships as are made of wood. And this is commonly their manner, thereby the sooner to pass the Cape: which our ship could not bear; so that we put back again with the wind, yet as little as we might, thereby to avoid the force of the sea, as much as we could.

But because the Pilot of the *San Thomas* trusted overmuch in her strength, and did purposely mean to be before us all, thereby, as he thought, to win the praise; the ship did, as it well appeared, lie still, and drive without any sails, which they call *payrar* [*drifting*]: and so, by the great force and strength of the seas, together with the overlading, was stricken in pieces and swallowed in the sea; both men, and all that was within her. As we might well perceive, coming to the Cape, by the swimming of whole chests, fats, balls, pieces of masts, dead men tied unto boards; and such like fearful tokens.

The other ships also that arrived in the island of Saint Helena, told us likewise that they had seen the like most pitiful sights; which was no small loss of so great treasure, and only many men. So that we, which beheld it, thought ourselves not free from the like danger. It was one of the richest ships that, in many years, had sailed out of India; and only by reason of the good report it had to be so good of sailing, being but new (for then it was but her second voyage), every man desired to go and lade their wares in her.

In the same ship, went Don PAULO DE LIMA PEREIRA, that raised the siege of Malacca, and had served the King thirty years in India, and had obtained many brave victories; thinking then to be in the top of his honour, and to be much advanced by the King. He also carried with him great treasure in jewels and other riches; also his wife, children, and one of his brethren: with many other gentlemen and soldiers that bare him company, thinking to have good fortune in their voyage.

There were likewise ten or twelve gentlewomen, some of them having their husbands in the ship; others, whose husbands were in Portugal. So that, to conclude, it was full of people, and most of the gentility of India: and in all our ships there were many, that seeing us in danger, would say that "they might have gone safely in the *San Thomas*," thinking it impossible that it should be cast away.

Therefore, it is manifestly seen that all the works and imaginations of men are but mere vanities; and that we must only put our trust in GOD: for that if GOD be not with us in our actions, all our labour is in vain.

But to return to our matter. Each ship did her best to be first, until the 17th of February; when we got before the *San Thomas*, being in 7° S.: and from that time forwards, we saw her no more; but only the tokens of her casting away about the Cape of Good Hope, which, after, when at the island of St. Helena, was told us more at large.

The same day, we had a great storm of wind and rain, so that the ruther of our great mast was broken by the force of the sea. From the line, we had a north and north-west wind, with continual rain, storms, and foul weather, never ceasing till we came to 20° S., which was upon the 25th of February. Then we had a south-east wind, called by the Portuguese the "General Wind" [*the Trade Wind*] with fairer weather: which they commonly find in 12° S., but we had it not before we were under 20° S. The cause whereof, we thought to be, that we had put so far into the sea, out of the common way. This wind commonly holdeth to 27° or 28° S., a little more or less: and then they must look for all kinds of winds and weathers, till they come to the Cape of Good Hope.

The 5th of March, being in 25° S., we had an East wind, with an exceeding great storm and rain; so that our rudder-staff [? *handle*] brake, and two more that we had in the ship, brake likewise, one after the other, on being put unto it; with the pin and joint wherein the end of the rudder hung: so we were forced to lie and drive, without steering, having struck all our sails; and the ship was so tossed by the waves on all sides, that we had not one dry place in all the ship. In this sort, we lay driving, for the space of two days and two nights together, with a continual storm and foul weather with rain.

The same night, we saw upon the mainyard and in many other places, a certain sign [*electrical sparks*] which the Portuguese call *Corpo Santo* or "the holy body of Brother PETER GONSALVES"; but the Spaniards call it *San Elmo*, and the Greeks (as ancient writers rehearse, and OVID among the rest) *Helle and Phryxus*. Whensoever that sign showeth upon the mast or mainyard or in any other place; it is commonly thought, that it is a sign of better weather. When they first perceive it, the Master or Chief Boatswain whistleth, and commandeth every man to salute it with *Salve, corpo santo!* and a, *Misericòrdia!* with a very great cry and exclamation.

This constellation, as astronomers do write, is engendered of great moisture and vapours; and showeth like a candle that burneth dimly, and skippeth from one place to another, never lying still. We saw five of them together, all like the light of a candle, which made me wonder; and I should have hardly believed it but that I saw it, and looked very earnestly upon it. And although it was foul weather, whereby I had no great leisure to think upon such curious things, yet I purposely came from under the hatches, to note it. Those five lights the Portuguese call *Coroa de nossa Senhora*, that is, "Our Lady's crown;" and have great hope therein, when they see it. And therewithal our men, being all in great fear and heaviness, began to revive again and to be glad; as if, thereby, they had been fully assured of better comfort.

The 7th of March, we had better weather; and then we took counsel how to mend our rudder. Some were of opinion, we should sail to Mozambique, and rule the rudder with a rope: others were of contrary opinion, and said we might mend it aboard, and so perform our voyage. So that, at the last, we pulled certain pieces out of the ship's side; for we had not brought one with us, as need required: but being pulled forth, they were all too little, and would not serve.

In the end, we found it convenient to take one of the bosses in our ship, and thereof, to make an anvil; and of two oxhides, a pair of bellows; wherewith we went to work: and of a piece of an old hook or drag, we took two or three ends whereof but one would serve, and that half broken; and the splinters, we bound with an iron hoop. So, it being fitted to the rudder; we set forwards, in the name of GOD.

This asked us two days' work, before we could despatch it; and we hoisted sail again, with great joy: and gave divers alms to Our Lady and the saints, with many promises of better life; as men, being in misery, commonly do.

The day after, we took the height of the sun, and found

ourselves to be in 28° 45°, and four hundred miles from the land of Natal. There, we had good weather, with a south-east wind.

Here is the hardest passage that is in all the voyage, and oftentimes they fear the land of Natal more than the Cape: for there, is commonly stormy and foul weather; and many ships have been spoiled and cast away there, as the Portuguese records can very well show. In the same part also, we found the signs of the casting away of the *San Thomas*. So that, to conclude, commonly the ships do there pay tribute, by casting some lading overboard, or else leave body and all behind.

For this cause, they never pass Natal without great fear; having a good watch and great foresight. All their ropes being stiff, and well looked unto. The pieces drawn in; all chests, pots, fats, and other roomage, that are not stowed under hatches, being thrown overboard into the sea: and everything settled, and made ready in his place. For in this coast they have one hour, fair weather: and another hour, stormy weather; in such manner, as if heaven and earth should waste and be consumed.

In that place likewise, with a clear and fair weather, there cometh a certain cloud, which, in show, seemeth no bigger than a man's fist, and therefore, by the Portuguese, is called *olho de boy* or "ox eye"; and although then it is clear and calm weather, and that the sails, for want of wind, do beat against the masts: yet as soon as they perceive that cloud, they must presently strike all their sails. For that, commonly, it is upon the ships, before they perceive it: and with such a storm and noise, that, without all doubt, it would strike a ship into the water, if there be not great care had to look unto it.

And it chanced to the Second Fleet, after the Portuguese had discovered the [East] Indies: there being ten or twelve ships in company, which, in such a calm and fair weather, let all their sails hang, and regarded them not. And this custom [*fact*], they observed in this their navigation. For suddenly the cloud came, with a most horrible storm, and fell upon them, before they could prevent [*prepare for*] it: whereby seven or eight were sunk in the seas, and never heard of again; and the rest, with great hurt and much danger, escaped. But, from that time forwards, they looked better to themselves; and have learned to know it: so that, at this present, they watch for it; and yet, it giveth them work enough to do.

The 12th of March, being in 31° S., we were right in the wind [*i.e., the wind was dead ahead*], and had a calm; whereupon we struck all our sails; and so lay driving four days together, which the Portuguese call *Payraes*: having a very high sea which tossed our ships in such sort, that the sailors esteem it to be worse than a storm. For there, the waves of the sea met in such sort on all sides, and clasped the ship in such a manner betwixt them; that they made all her ribs to crack and in a manner to open: so that it is very dangerous for the ship.

We were in very great care [*fear*] for our Fouke mast; and therefore we bound our masts and all the ship about cables, as hard as we possibly might.

This continued to the 17th of March, and then we had a little wind; so that we hoisted sail again: but it continued no longer than to the next day.

Then we fell again into the wind, and had a storm; wherewith our mainyard broke: and then again we struck all our sails; and so lay driving or *payraer*-ing, as the Portuguese call it.

In the meantime, we mended our mainyard; and so we continued driving without our sails till the 20th of March: with great risings of the waves of the sea, which tormented us; as in that place they commonly do. All which time we were in 31° S., and could not pass forward.

In that time, we saw many birds, which the Portuguese call *Antenalen*, and are as big as ducks.

The 20th of March, we had a little wind, but very sharp; yet we hoisted our sails, and sailed by the wind.

The next night after, we had a calm; which continued till the 22nd: and then we fell again into the wind, with so great a storm that we were compelled to strike all our sails, which we could hardly pull in; and could not stay the ship in any sort, it drave so fast. Whereby we were in great danger, so that we were compelled to bind the bonnet about the Forecastle, which was our sail (for other sail we might not bear); and so sailed backwards whither the wind would drive us, thereby to have some ease. Yet we had enough to do, for we were compelled to throw our great boat overboard; with all chests, pots, and vessels that stood upon the hatches, with other wares, such as came first to hand.

This storm continued for the space of two days and three nights, without ceasing.

The 25th of March, being the day before Palm Sunday [*N.S.*], we had better wind and weather, after we had given great alms to our blessed Lady of the Annunciation, whose feast was upon that day; and again hoisted up our sails, keeping our course towards the Cape.

At the same time, we had a disease [? *scurvy*] in our ship, that took us in the mouth, lips, throat, and tongue; which took off the skin and made them swell: whereby they could not eat but with great pain; and not one in the ship but had it.

The 8th of April, in the morning, after we had sailed fifteen days before the wind, towards the Cape, we perceived a sign of the land, which was green water: but we found no ground; yet was it not above forty miles from the land, according to the Pilot's judgement.

We saw there also divers of the birds, called *Mangas de velludo*, that is, "Velvet sleeves"; for they have upon the ends of their wings, black points like velvet; all the rest being white and somewhat grey: which they hold for a certain sign of land, that lieth within the Cape of Good Hope, called *Baya de la Goa*, or "the Bay of the Lake" in 33½° S.

The 9th of April, at night, we were again right in the wind, in 35° 30′ S., with a great storm and foul weather, that continued till the 14th of the same month: so that we were compelled (not being able to endure the force of the sea, with the continual storm and foul weather) to sail back again before the wind, with the half of our Fouke sail up. For we found ourselves not strong enough to drive without sails, as the ship commonly used to do, which oftentimes is the cause of their casting away: as it may well be judged by reason of the great force and strength of the waves that run there, so that it seemeth almost impossible for a ship to bear out so great a force, though it were of iron.

And though we sailed [backward] before the wind, yet we

had danger enough; for the sea came behind and over our ship, and filled all the hatches: whereby we were compelled to bind our masts, cables, and all the ship round about with ropes; that, with the great force of the sea, it might not stir, and fly to pieces. And we were forced to pump, night and day.

We had at each end of the Fouke-yard, a rope that reached to the Pilot: and at each rope, there stood fifteen or sixteen men: the Pilot sitting in his seat; and the under Pilot behind, upon the stern of the ship [*which was now going backwards, stern first*] to mark the course of the sea, and so to advertise the other Pilot. At the rudder, there stood ten or twelve men; and the other sailors upon the hatches, to rule the sails.

As the waves came and covered the ship, the Under Pilot called, and then the Chief Pilot spake to them at the rudder "to hold stiff!" and commanded the ropes that were at the Fouke-yard to be pulled stiff. The sailors and the Chief Boatswain likewise standing on the hatches, to keep the ship right in the waves: for if the waves had once gotten us about that they had entered on the sides of the ship, it had been certainly said of us, *requiescant in pace*. And it was there, almost as cold as it is here with us [*in Holland*] in winter, when it freezeth not. Whereby we were all sore toiled, and in a manner out of heart; so that we esteemed ourselves clean cast away.

For we were forced, by turns, not one excepted, to go to the rudder, and from thence to the pump; so that we had no time to sleep, eat, rest, nor clothe ourselves. And to help us the better, the staff [? *handle*] of our rudder brake in pieces, and had almost slain two or three of our men: but GOD had pity on us; so that there happened no other hurt, but that some of them were a little amazed [*stunned*].

This continued till the 14th of April, without any change; whereupon all the Officers of the ship assembled, together with others of the company, taking counsel what was best to be done: and perceiving the ship not to be strong enough to pass the Cape, they concluded, by *Protestation* whereunto they subscribed their hands, to sail with the ship to Mozambique, and there to winter and to repair the ship, and provide all necessaries for it.

Which greatly grieved the common sort, because they did find as great danger in turning back again to Mozambique, as to pass the Cape; for they were to sail again by the land of Natal, which they feared as much as the Cape. And also, though they did arrive at Mozambique, yet they accounted it as much as a lost voyage. For they must stay there till next year, and spend there all they have; for all things that come thither, are brought out of India, so that everything there is as dear as gold: which would be hard for the poor sailors and swabers, having but little means to relieve themselves; and thereby they should be constrained to sell that little they had brought with them for half the value. Besides that, they were then about 500 miles from Mozambique.

Wherefore, there grew a great noise and murmuring in the ship, that cursed the Captain and Officers, because the ship was badly provided: for it had not one rope more than hung about the ship; nor anything whereof to make them, if those that we had, should have chanced to break.

The Captain laid the fault on the Master, because he asked not for them, when he was at land. The Master said that he had spoken for them, and that the *cairo* or hemp, whereof ropes are made in India, was delivered to the Captain; and that he had sold the best part thereof, to put the money in his purse: and that was the cause why we wanted.

With this disorder, they bring their matters to pass, not once remembering what may fall out: but when they are in danger; then, there is nothing else but crying *Misericordia!* and calling to "Our Lady" for help.

The Captain could not tell what to answer, seeing us in that trouble; but said that "He marvelled at nothing so much, as why our LORD GOD suffered them (being so good Christians and Catholics as they were) to pass the Cape with so great torments and dangerous weather, having so great and strong ships: and that the Englishmen (being heretics, and blasphemers of GOD) passed the Cape so easily, with such small and weak vessels." For they had received news in India, that an English ship [? *DRAKE's* Pelican, *on 18th June 1580: or CAVENDISH's ship, the* Desire, *eleven months before, viz., on the 19th of May 1588, see Vol. I. p. 293*] had passed the Cape, with very great ease.

So we made back again towards Mozambique, being in great despair; for no man cared to lay his hand to work, and hardly any man would obey the Officers of the ship. Sailing in this manner, we perceived divers vessels [*casks, &c.*], and boards with dead men bound upon them, driving in the sea: which comforted us a little, we thinking that some of the other ships were in the same taking; and had thrown some of their goods overboard, and so made towards Mozambique before us: whereby we thought to have company, and that we were not alone unfortunate; for it is commonly said that "companions in misery are a comfort to one another," and so it was to us. But, I would to GOD! it had been so, as we imagined; but it was far worse than turning back again: for those were the signs of the casting away of the *San Thomas*; as we were afterwards advertised in the island of Saint Helena.

The 15th of April we had another great calm; which continued till the 17th: and taking the height of the sun, we found ourselves to be 37° S., to the great admiration [*astonishment*] of all the company. For being, as I said, in 35° S., and having sailed for the space of five days, with so great a wind and stormy weather, we should rather, by all men's reason, have lessened our degrees; and by estimation, we made account to have been in 30° S., or 32° S. at the highest. The cause why our ship went backward, in that sort, against wind and weather, towards the Cape, thinking we made towards Mozambique, was by the water, which in those countries carrieth with a very strong stream [*current*] towards the Cape: as the Pilot told us he had proved at other times; yet he thought not that the water had run with so great a stream as now, by experience, he found it did.

So as it seemed that GOD, miraculously (against man's reason and judgement, and all the force of wind and storms), would have us pass the Cape, when we were least in hope thereof: whereby we may plainly perceive that all men's actions, without the hand of GOD, are of no moment.

The same day, we again saw green water, and the birds called *Mangas de velludo* or "Velvet sleeves;" which are certain signs of the Cape of Good Hope: and, about evening, a swallow flew into our ship, whereat they much rejoiced, saying that "It was a sign and foreshowing that Our Lady had sent the swallow on board to comfort us; and that we should pass the Cape." Wherewith they once again agreed to prove if we could pass it; seeing we had had such signs and tokens to put us in good comfort that GOD would help us. This being concluded [*settled*], we sang the *Litany* with *Ora pro nobis!* and gave many alms; with promises of pilgrimages and visitations and such like things, which was our daily work.

With that, the sailors and others began to take courage and to be lusty, every one willingly doing his office: offering rather to lose life and welfare in adventuring to pass the Cape; than, with full assurance of their safety, to return to Mozambique. We had then great waves, and very big water in the sea: which left us not, till we came to the other side of the Cape.

The 18th of April, we fell again into the wind, with as great storms and foul weather as ever we had before; so that we verily thought we should have been cast away: for at every minute, the sea covered our ship with water. To lighten her, we cast overboard divers chests, and much cinnamon, with other things that first came to hand. Wherewith every man made account to die; and began to confess themselves, and to ask each other's forgiveness: thinking, without more hope, that our last day was come. This storm continued in this sort, at the least, for the space of twenty-four hours. In the meantime great alms were given in our ship to many Virgin *Maries* and other saints; with great devotion and promises of other wonderful things, when they came to land. At the last, GOD comforted us, and sent us better weather. For, on the 19th of April, the weather began to clear up; and therewith, we were in better comfort.

The 20th of April, we took the height of the sun, and found it to be 36° S.: and again we saw green water, some birds which they call *Alcatraces* [*i.e.*, *albatrosses*], and many sea-wolves; which they hold for certain signs of the Cape of Good Hope. We were, as we thought, hard by the land; but yet saw none. The same day, we had the wind somewhat fuller, and were in great hope to pass the Cape: so that the men began to be in better comfort, by reason of the signs we had seen.

All that day, we saw green water, till the 22nd of April, upon which day, twice, and in the night following, we cast out the lead, and found no ground: which is a good sign that we had passed the Cape *das Aquilhas*, or "the Cape of Needles," which lieth in 35° S., about twenty miles from the

Cape of Good Hope in 34° 30′ S. As about this Cape *das Aquilhas*, ground is found, at the least, thirty or forty miles from the land, we knew we were past it: and also by the colour of the water, and the birds which are always found there. And the better to assure us, the great and high sea that had so long tormented us, left us; and then we found a smoother water, much differing from the former: so that we then seemed to have come out of hell into paradise, with as great joy as if we thought we were within the sight of some haven. And had withal, a good wind; though somewhat cold.

The 23rd of April, we passed the Cape of Good Hope, with a great and general gladness; it being then three months and three days after we had set sail from Cochin: not once seeing any land or sands [*shoals*] at all, but only the assured tokens of the said Cape; which happeneth very seldom, for the Pilots do always use what means they can to see the Cape and to know the land, to certainly know thereby that they are past it. For then, their degrees must lessen; and then they may as soon [*hap to*] make towards Mozambique as to the island of St. Helena. For although they can well perceive it by the water, yet is it necessary for them to see the land, the better to set their course unto St. Helena: wherein they must always keep on the left hand; otherwise it were impossible for them to come at it, if they leave that course. For if they once pass it, they cannot come to it again: because there bloweth continually but one kind of wind, which is south-east [*Trade Wind*]. Thus having passed the Cape, we got before the wind.

The 24th of April, the Pilot willed us to give *bona viagen* unto the Cape of Good Hope, according to the custom: which was done with great joy and gladness, by all that were in the ship. For then, they assure themselves that they sail to Portugal, and shall not turn again into India: for so long as they are not past the Cape, they are always in doubt. We were then about 50 miles beyond the Cape.

The signs and tokens whereby they know themselves to have certainly passed the Cape, are great heaps and pieces of thick reeds that always thereabouts drive upon the water, at least 15 or 20 miles from the land; also certain birds called by the Portuguese, *Feisoins*, somewhat greater than seamews, being white and full of black spots all over their bodies; and are very easy to be known from all other birds.

Having passed the Cape, the Pilots set their course for St. Helena, north-west, and north-west-by-west.

The 27th of April, we were right in the wind, and so continued till the next day; and then we had a calm, being in 30° S. on the Portugal side.

The 29th of April, we got before the General Wind [*the Trade Wind*] that always bloweth in those countries, all the whole year, until you come to the Equinoctial line: so that they may well let their sails stand, and lay them down to sleep; for, in the greatest wind that bloweth there, they need not strike their mainyard, above half the mast.

The 12th of May, in the morning, betimes, we discovered the island of St. Helena: whereat there was as great joy in the ship, as if we had been in heaven. We were then about two miles from the land, the island lying from us west-south-west; whereunto we sailed so close that, with a caliver shot, we might reach unto the shore. Being hard by it, we sailed about a corner of land that lay north-west from us, which having compassed, we sailed close by the land, west-north-west: the land on that side being so high and steep that it seemed to be a wall that reached to the skies.

In that sort, we sailed [on the north side of the island] about a mile and a half, and compassed about the other corner that lay westward from us: which corner being compassed, we presently perceived the ships that lay in the road; which were those ships that set sail before us out of India. They were lying about a small half mile from the foresaid corner, close under the land; so that as the land there lieth south-east from them, by reason of the high land, the ships lie there as safe as if they were in a haven. For they may well hear the wind whistle on the tops of their mainyards; but lower it cannot come: and they lie so close under the land, that they may almost cast a stone upon the shore.

There is good ground there at 25 and 30 fathoms deep; but if they chance to put further out or to pass beyond it; they must go forward, for they can get no more unto the land. For this cause we kept so close to the shore, that the height of the land took the wind from us; and as the ship would not steer without wind, so it drave upon the land: whereby our boresprit [*bowsprit*] touched the shore; and therewith, we thought that ship and goods had all been cast away. But, by reason of the great depth, being ten fathoms, of water; and, with the help of the boats and men of the other ships that came unto us, we put off from the land, without any hurt: and by those boats, we were brought to a place where the other ships lay at anchor; which is right against a valley, that lieth between two high hills, wherein there standeth a little church, called Saint Helena.

There we found five ships, which were, the ship that came from Malacca; and the *Santa Maria*, which had been there about fifteen days [*i.e., had arrived 27th of April*]: both of which came together to the Cape of Good Hope. The *Sant Antonio*, and the *San Christopher*, the admiral, that had arrived there ten days before [*i.e., on 2nd of May*]: and the *Nostra Señora de Concepcao*, which came thither but the day before us [*i.e.*, 11*th of May*]. So that there wanted none of the fleet, but the *San Thomas*; and, by the signs and tokens that we and the other ships had seen at sea (as masts, deals, fats, chests, and many dead men that had bound themselves upon boards; with a thousand other such like signs), we presumed to be lost: as we after understood, for it was never seen after[wards].

Our admiral [*flag ship*] likewise, had been in great danger of casting away. For, although it was a new ship, and this the first voyage it had made; yet it was so eaten with worms, that it had, at the least, 20 handsful deep of water within it. At the Cape, they were forced to throw half of the goods overboard into the sea; and were constrained continually to pump with two pumps, both night and day, and never hold still. And being at the island of St. Helena, she had there also sunk to the ground, if the other ships had not helped her.

The rest of the ships could likewise tell what dangers and miseries they had endured.

About three months before our arrival at St. Helena [*i.e., in February* 1589] there had been a ship, which, the year before, set out of Ormus, with the goods and men that remained of the *San Salvador* at Zanzibar, that had been saved by the Portuguese army, and brought to Ormus, as in another place I have declared [*see p.* 44]. That ship had wintered in Mozambique, and had passed by the Cape very soon; and so sailed, without any company, to Portugal. She left some of her sick men on the island, as the manner is; which the next ships that come thither, must take into them.

These gave us intelligence that four [*or rather eleven*] months before our arrival, there had been an English ship [*CAVENDISH's ship the* Desire, *see Vol. I. p.* 293] at the island of St. Helena, which had sailed through the Straits of Magellan, and through the South Seas, and from thence, to the Philippine Islands; and had passed through the Straits of Sunda, that lie beyond Malacca, between the islands of Sumatra and Java: in the which way, she had taken a ship of China, such as they call *Junks*, ladened with silver and gold, and all kinds of silks. And that, she sent a letter, with a small present, to the Bishop of MALACCA, telling him, "That she sent him that of friendship, meaning to come herself and visit him."

Out of that ship of China, they took a Portuguese Pilot; and so passed the Cape of Good Hope, and came to the island of St. Helena: where they took in fresh water and other necessaries, and beat down the altar and cross that stood in the church.

They left behind them a kettle and a sword, which the Portuguese, at our arrival, found there: yet could they not conceive or think what that might mean? Some thought it was left there for a sign to some other ships of his company; but every man may think, what he will thereof.

In the ship of Malacca came for Factor of the Pepper one GERRARD VAN AFHUISEN, born in Antwerp, and dwelling in Lisbon: who had sailed from Lisbon, in the same ship, about two years before. For they had stayed in Malacca, at the least, fourteen months; by reason of the wars and troubles that were in that country, until Malacca was relieved as I said before [*pp.* 42-46]: whereby they had passed great misery, and been at great charges. And because it is a very unwholesome country, together with the constant lying there so long; of 200 men that at first sailed from Lisbon in the ship, there were but 18 or 20 left alive: so that they were enforced to take in other unskilful men, in Malacca, to bring the ship home.

This GERRARD VAN AFHUISEN, being of mine acquaintance, and my good friend before my departure out of Portugal for India, marvelled and joyed much to find me there, little thinking that we should meet in so strange a place: and there, we discoursed of our past travels.

And of him, among divers other things, I learned many true instructions, as well of Malacca as of the countries and islands lying about it; both as to their manner of dealing in trade or merchandise, as in other memorable things.

St. Helena to Lisbon.

THE Island of St. Helena is six miles in compass, and lieth in 16° 15′ S.

It is a very high and hilly country, so that it commonly reacheth unto the clouds. The country itself is very ashy and dry. Also all the trees (whereof there is a great store, and grow of themselves in the woods) that are therein, are little worth, but only to burn.

When the Portuguese first discovered it [*on 21st May* 1502], there were not any beasts or fruits at all within the island; but only a great store of freshwater. This is excellently good, and falleth down from the mountains, and so runneth, in great abundance, into the valley where the Church standeth; and from thence, by small channels in the sea, where the Portuguese fill their vessels full of water, and wash their clothes. So that it is a great benefit for them; and a pleasant sight it is to behold, how clear, and in how many streams, the water runneth down the valley: which may be thought a miracle considering the dryness of the country, together with the stony rocks and hills therein.

The Portuguese have, by little and little, brought many beasts into it; and planted all sorts of fruits in the valleys: which have grown there in so great abundance, that it is almost incredible. For it is so full of goats, bucks, wild hogs, hens, partridges, and doves, by thousands, that any man that that will, may hunt and take them. There would be always plenty and sufficient, although there came as many ships more to the island as there do: and they may kill them with stones and staves, by reason of the great numbers of them.

Now for fruits, as Portuguese figs, pomegranates, oranges, lemons, citrons, and such like fruits; there are so many that grow without planting or setting, that all the valleys are full of them: which is a great pleasure to behold, so that it seemeth to be an earthly Paradise. It hath fruit all the year long, because it raineth there, by showers, at the least five or six times every day; and then again, the sun so shineth that whatsoever is planted there, it groweth very well. But, because the Portuguese are not over curious of new things, there groweth not of all sorts of fruits of Portugal and India in that island. For assuredly, without any doubt, they would grow well in that land, because of the good temperature of the air.

Besides this, they have so great abundance of fish round about the island, that it seemeth a wonder wrought of GOD; for, with crooked nails, they may take as much fish as they will: so that all the ships do provide themselves with fish of all sorts in that place, which is hung up and dried; and is of as good a taste and savour as any fish that I ever ate, and this every man, that hath been there, affirmeth to be true.

And the better to serve their turns; upon the rocks, they find salt, which serveth them for their necessary provisions.

So that, to conclude, it is an earthly Paradise for the Portuguese ships; and seemeth to have been miraculously discovered for the refreshing and service of the same: considering the smallness and highness of the land, lying in the middle of the Ocean seas, and so far from the firm land or any other islands, that it seemeth to be a Buoy placed in the middle of the Spanish seas. For if this island were not, it were impossible for the ships to make any good or prosperous voyage. For it hath often fallen out, that some ships which have missed thereof, have endured the greatest misery in the world; and were forced to put into the coast of Guinea, there to stay the falling of the rain, and so to get fresh water; and afterwards came, half dead and spoiled, to Portugal.

It is the fashion, that all the sick persons that are in the ships, and cannot well sail in them, are left there in the island; with some provision of rice, biscuit, oil, and spices: for fish and flesh, they may have enough. For when the ships are gone, then all the beasts (which, by reason of the great number of people, fly into the mountains) come down again into the valleys; where they may take them with their hands, and kill them as they list.

These sick men stay there till the next year, till other ships come hither, which take them with them. They are commonly soon healed in that island, it being a very sound and pleasant country: and it is very seldom seen that any of them die there, because they have always a temperate air and cool wind, and always fruit throughout the whole year.

The King will not suffer any man to dwell in it, because they should not destroy and spoil the country, and hold it as their own: but will have it common for every man to take what he hath need of.

In time past, there dwelt an hermit in the isle, under pretence of doing penance, and to uphold the Church. He killed many of the goats and bucks: so that, every year, he sold at the least 500 or 600 skins, and made great profit thereon; which the King hearing, caused him presently to be brought from thence to Portugal.

Likewise, upon a time, two Kaffirs or black people of Mozambique, and a Javanese, with two women slaves, stole out of the ships; and hid themselves in the rocks of this island, which are very high and wild, whereby men can hardly pass them. They lived there together, and begat children, so that, in the end, there were, at the least, twenty persons: who, when the ships were gone, ran throughout the island, and did much hurt; making their houses and dwelling-places between some of the hills where not any of the Portuguese had been, nor yet could easily come at them, and therein they hid themselves till the ships were gone. But, in the end, they were perceived, and the Portuguese used all the means they could to take them: but they knew so well how to hide and defend themselves that, in many years, they could not be taken. In the end, fearing that in time they might be hurtful unto them and hinder them much; by express commandment of the King, after long and great labour, they took them all, and brought them prisoners to Portugal.

So that, at this present, no man dwelleth therein; but only the sick men, as I told you before.

When the ships come thither, every man maketh his lodging under a tree, setting a tent about it; and the trees are there so thick, that it presently seemeth a little town or an army in the field. Every man provideth for himself, flesh, fish, fruit, and wood; for there is enough for them all: and every one washeth linen.

There, they hold a General Fasting and Prayer, with *Mass* every day: which is done with great devotion, with procession, and thanksgiving, and other hymns; thanking GOD, that He hath preserved them from the danger of the Cape of Good Hope, and brought them to that island in safety.

They use oftentimes to carve their names and marks in trees and plants, for a perpetual memory: whereof many hundreds are there to be found; which letters, with the growing of the trees, do also grow bigger and bigger.

We found names that had been there since the years 1510 and 1515, and every year following, orderly; which names stood upon fig trees, every letter being of the bigness of a span, by reason of the age and growing of the trees.

This shall suffice for the description of the island of St. Helena.

The 21st of May [*N.S.*], being Saint Helena's Day and Whitsunday, after we had taken in all our fresh water and other necessaries, we set sail altogether in company, and directed our course towards Portugal: leaving about fifteen sick men in the island, and some slaves that ran out of the ships.

The 26th of May, in the evening, we spoke with the *Santa Maria*, and the next day [*27th of May*] with the Galleon of Malacca. The same morning, and in the afternoon, with the Admiral; who willed us to follow him unto the Island of Ascension.

The same day, [*27th*] one of our slaves fell overboard, and although we used all the means we could to save him; yet we could not do it, by reason we sailed before the wind.

The same day, at night, we saw the island of Ascension; and lavered [*tacked*] all that night, because we would not pass the island.

In the morning of the 28th of May, we sailed about the island, to see if there were any ground to anchor on: because the Admiral was so leaky, that she could no longer hold out. Her men had desired the Officers of the ship that they would lay the goods on land in the island of Ascension, and there leave it with good watch and necessaries for them that kept it; and so sail with the empty ship to Portugal and there procure some other ship to fetch the goods: thinking it was sufficient to have it well watched and kept there; for that there cometh not a ship in twenty years into that island, because there is nothing to be had in it.

We went close unto it, by a very white and fair sand, where the Admiral and all the ships cast out the lead, and found from 80 to 50 and 40 fathoms of water. And although they might have gone closer to the land, yet the Officers excused themselves, saying, "That they could not go nearer, and that it was too deep, and very dangerous for them to anchor there," which they said to pacify the men; desiring that they might borrow two pumps more of the other ships, and so, without doubt, they could bring the ship safe to Portugal. And although it would be great pain and labour for them to do it, yet they must, of force, content themselves: for the Admiral and all the gentlemen that were in the ship, pumped both day and night, as their turns came about, as well as the meanest; only to encourage the people.

They borrowed one pump of the *Santa Maria*; and sent to desire us to lend them another. Although our ship was none of the best among the fleet, and we were of opinion not to lend them any (not knowing what need we should have ourselves, having so long a way to sail): yet, in the end, seeing the great necessity they were in; we lent them one: the rather because they said that "The admiral's meaning was, if it were calm weather, to discharge some of their wares into other ships; thereby to lighten themselves": but it fell not out as they thought; so that, with great misery and labour, they overcame their voyage.

This island lieth in 8° 30′ S. There is not any fresh water in it, nor one green leaf or branch. It hath certain fair and white sands about it; and a great store of fish, wherein it surpasseth St. Helena.

From that island, the ships hold their course north-west-by-west, to 1° N., where there lieth a cliff [*rock*] called *Penedo de Sam Pedro*; which many times they see. It is 300 miles from the island of Ascension.

The 5th of June, we again passed the Equinoctial line, and then again began to see the North Star.

The 8th of June, being 4° N., we lost our General South-east Wind, that had served us from the Cape of Good Hope hither.

Then began the rains and calms, for then we began to come near the coast of Guinea; which continueth to 9° N. These calms and rains held us till 11° N., being the 20th of June.

The ships separated themselves, by reason of the calms, which made them not able to stir: and in 11° N., they met again.

There we had a north-east wind, which is called a General Wind, because it floweth continually in those countries; and holdeth to 30° N., and 32° N.; beginning many times at 6° N., and 7° N., be it we had it not, till we were in 11° N. This wind is somewhat scant; for we must, of force, sail in the wind, because our chief course is north-west-by-north.

The 23rd of June, we passed Cape de Verde, in 15° N.

The 26th of the same month, we passed the Islands of Cape de Verde, which are ten in number.

Then we entered into the *Sargasso* Sea, which is all covered with herbs, so that it seemeth to be like a green field; and so thick that a man cannot see the water, neither can the ships passed through it, but with great labour, unless they have a strong wind. The herb is like samphire, of a yellow colour; and hath berries like gooseberries, but nothing in them. The Portuguese call it *Sargasso*, because it is like the herb *Sargasso*, that groweth in their wells in Portugal. It is not known whence it cometh: for there is no land nor island known to be near that sea, but the coast of Africa, which is 400 miles from thence. It is thought that it cometh from the ground; and yet there is no ground in that place to be found.

In sailing to India, the ships come not into that sea; for then they keep closer to the shore, so that it is not once seen: and it is not found in any place but there, from 20° N. to 34° N., so thick and so full, as if they were whole islands, most strange to behold. In that country, it is as cold in winter as it is here with us [*in Holland*], when it freezes not:

which the Portuguese esteem a great cold; and clothe themselves against it, as we do in a mighty great frost.

The 2nd of July, we were in the height [*latitude*] of the Canary Islands, in 28° N. and 29° N.; which lay on our right hand.

The 6th of July, we were under 32° N., where we lost the General North-east Wind, and had a calm, and saw much of the *Sargasso*, which covered all the sea.

The 10th of the same month, we got again before the wind, being in 34° N.; and then, we saw no more of the *Sargasso* herb, but a fair clear sea.

The 18th of July, we were in 39° N., under which height lieth the islands of Corvo and Terceira; and the river of Lisbon: all these days we had many calms.

The next day, we had a west wind, being a right fore wind; and saw many flying fishes, almost as great as haddocks; that flew four or five fathoms high above the water.

The 22nd of July [*N.S.*], the wind continuing, about noon, we saw the islands of Flores and Corvo, which lie close to one another. From thence, it is 70 miles Eastward, to the island of Terceira.

At that time, we began to have many sick men, that is to say, some sick in their eyes, and some in their breasts and bellies, by reason of the long voyage, and because their victuals began to loose their taste and savour. Many wanted meat [*i.e., had no animal food*]: whereby divers of them, through want, were compelled to seethe rice with salt water. So that some of them died; which, many times, were found under the fore deck, that had lain dead two or three days, no man knowing it: which was a pitiful sight to behold, considering the misery they endured aboard those ships.

There died in our ship, from India unto that place, of slaves and others, to the number of twenty-four persons.

The same day, about evening, being by the islands of Flores and Corvo, we perceived three ships that made towards us, which came from under the land: which put us in great fear, for they came close by our admiral, and shot divers times at him, and at another ship of our company; whereby we perceived them to be Englishmen (for they bare an English flag upon their maintop), but none of them showed to be about 60 tons in greatness [*while the size of each Carrack was from* 600 *to* 1,600 *tons*]. About evening, they followed after us: and all night, bore lanterns with candles burning in them at their sterns, although the moon shined.

The same night, we passed hard by the island of Fayal. The next day [23*rd*], being betwixt the island of St. George that lay on our right hand, and the small island of Gracioso on our left hand; we espied the three English ships, still following us, take counsel together: whereof one sailed backwards (thinking that some other ship had come after us without company), and, for a small time, was out of sight; but it was not long before it came again to the other two.

Wherewith they took counsel, and all three came together against our ship, because we lay in the lee of all the ships, and had the island of St. George on the one side instead of a sconce [*bulwark*], thinking so to deal with us that, in the end, we should be constrained to run upon the shore; whereof we wanted not much.

In that manner, with their flags openly displayed, they came lustily towards us, sounding their trumpets; and sailed at least three times about us, beating [*firing at*] us with musket and caliver, and some great pieces; which did not hurt us in the body of our ship, but spoiled all our sails and ropes. And to conclude, we were so plagued by them that no man durst put forth his head; and when we shot off a piece, we had at the least an hour's work to lade it again; whereby we had as great a noise and cry in the ship as if we had been cast away: whereat the Englishmen themselves began to mock us; and with a thousand jesting words called unto us.

In the meantime, the other ships hoisted all their sails, and did the best they could to sail to the island of Terceira; not looking once behind them to help us, and doubting [*fearing*] they should come too late thither: not caring for us, but thinking themselves to have done sufficiently, so they saved their own stakes; whereby it may easily be seen, what company they keep one with the other, and what order is among them.

In the end, the Englishmen, perceiving small advantage against us (little knowing in what case and fear we were), and also because we were not far from Terceira, left us; which made us not a little to rejoice, as thinking ourselves to be risen from death to life: although we were not well assured, neither yet void of fear, till we lay in the road before Terceira, and under the safety of the Portuguese fort; and we made all the sails we could, that we might get thither in good time.

On the other side, we were in great doubt, because we knew not what they did in the island, nor whether they were our friends or enemies; and we doubted so much the more, because we found no Men of war, nor any Caravels of Advices from Portugal, as we made our accounts to do, than they might convoy us from thence, or give us advice as they, ordinarily, in that country, use to do: and because the Englishmen had been so victorious in those parts, it made us suspect that it went not well with Spain.

They of the island of Terceira were in no less fear than we were: for seeing our fleet, they thought us to be English, and that we came to overrun the island; because the three Englishmen had bound up their flags, and came in company with us. For which cause, the island sent out two Caravels that lay there with Advices from the King, for the Indian ships that should come thither. Those caravels came to view us, and perceiving what we were, made after us; whereupon the English ships left us, and made towards them, as the caravels thought them to be friends and shunned them not, as supposing them to be of our company: but we shot four or five times, and made signs unto them, that they should make towards the island; which they presently did.

The Englishmen perceiving that, did put forwards into the sea. So the caravels boarded us, telling us, "That the men of the island were all in arms, having received advice from Portugal, that Sir FRANCIS DRAKE was in readiness, and would come unto those islands."

They likewise brought us news of the overthrow of the Spanish fleet [*the Armada in* 1588] before England; and that the Englishmen had been before the gates of Lisbon [*with Don ANTONIO, and under Sir F. DRAKE and Sir JOHN NORRIS, in May* 1589]: whereupon the King gave us commandment that we should put into the island of Terceira; and there lie under the safety of the Castle until we received further advices what we should do, or whither we should sail. For they thought it too dangerous for us to go to Lisbon.

This news put our fleet in great fear, and made us look upon each other, not knowing what to say. It being dangerous for the ships to put into the road, because it lieth open to the sea: so that the Indian ships, although they had express commandment from the King, yet durst not anchor there: but used only to lavere [*tack*] to and fro; sending their boats on land to fetch such necessaries as they wanted, without anchoring.

But being by necessity compelled thereunto, as also by the King's commandment; and because we understood the Earl of CUMBERLAND not to be far from those islands with certain ships of war [*the Earl did not arrive at the Azores, till the* 11*th August, N.S. see p.* 188]: we made necessity a virtue, and entering the road, anchored close under the Castle, staying for advices and order from the King to perform our voyage; it being then the 24th [*N.S., i.e., O.S.* 14*th*] of July and St. James's Day.

We were in all six ships, that is, five from the East Indies and one from Malacca; and lay in the road, before the town of Angra: from whence we presently sent three or four caravels to Portugal, with advices unto the King of our arrival.

There we lay in great danger and much fear; for when the month of August cometh, it is very dangerous lying before that island: for then it beginneth to storm. The ships are there safe from all winds, saving the south and south-east winds; but when they blow, they lie in a thousand dangers: especially the East India ships, which are very heavily ladened and so full that they are almost ready to sink; so that they can hardly be steered.

The 4th of August, in the night, we had a south wind out of the sea, wherewith it began so to storm, that all the ships were in great danger to be cast away, and to run upon the shore: so that they were in great fear; and shot off their pieces to call for help. The officers and most of the sailors were on land; and none but pugs [? *boys*] and slaves in the ships: for it is a common custom with the Portuguese, that wheresoever they anchor, presently they go all on land, and let the ship lie with a boy or two in it.

All the bells of the town were hereupon rung, and there

was such a noise and cry in every place, that one could not hear the other speak. Those that were on land, by reason of the foul weather, could not get aboard; and they in the ship could not come to land. Our ship, the *Santa Cruz*, was in great danger, thinking verily it should have run on the sands: but GOD helped them.

The ship that came from Malacca brake her cables; and had not men enough aboard the ship, nor any that could tell how to cast forth another anchor; so that, in the end, they cut their masts, and drave upon the cliffs, where it stayed and brake in pieces, and presently sank under the water to the upper orlop. With that, the wind came north-west, wherewith the storm ceased; and the water became calm. If that had not been, ail the ships had followed the same course; for some of them were at the point to cut their masts and cables to save their lives: but GOD would not have it so.

In that ship of Malacca, was lost much rich and costly merchandise; for these ships are ordinarily as rich as any ships that come from India, being full of all the rich wares of China, Moluccas, Japan, and all those countries: so that it was a great pity to see what costly things (as silks, damasks, cloths of gold and silver, and such like wares) fleeted upon the sea, and were torn in pieces.

There were much goods saved, that lay in the upper part of the ship, and also by duckers [*divers*], as pepper, nutmegs, and cloves; but most of it was lost: and that which was saved, was, in a manner, spoiled, and little worth; which was presently, by the King's Officers in the island, was seized upon and to the Farmers' uses, shut up in the *Alsandega* or Custom House, for the King's custom. Not once regarding the poor men, nor their long and dangerous voyage that had continued the space of three years, with so great misery and trouble endured by them at Malacca, as in another place [*pp.* 42-46] I have already showed; so that they could not obtain so much favour of the King nor of his Officers, that they might have some part of the goods that were saved and brought to land, although they offered to put in sureties for so much as the custom might amount to, or else to leave as much goods in the Officer's hands as would satisfy them.

And although they made daily and pitiful complaints that

they had not wherewith to live; and that they desired, upon their own adventure, to freight certain ships or caravels at their own charge, and to put in good sureties to deliver the goods in the Custom House of Lisbon; yet could they not obtain their requests, but were answered, that "The King, for the assurance of his custom and of all the goods; would send an *armado* by sea to fetch the goods": which "fetching" continued for the space of two years and a half; and yet nothing was done, for there came no *armado*.

In the meantime, the poor sailors consumed all they had; and desperately cursed themselves, the King, and all his Officers. Yet, in the end, by the great and unfortunate suit of the Farmers of the Pepper, every man had license to lade his goods in what ship he would, after it had lain there for the space of two years and a half; putting in sureties to deliver the goods into the Custom House of Lisbon, where they must pay the half or more of the same goods for custom to the King: without any respect of their hard fortune and great misery, during their long and dangerous voyage.

And he that will be despatched in the Custom House there, must fee the Officers; otherwise it is most commonly three or four months before the goods are delivered unto the owners: and the best things, or any fine device that the Merchants, for their own uses, bring out of India, if the Officers like them, they must have them; yet they will promise to pay for them, but they set no day when. So the poor Merchants are forced to give them the rest; and are well contented that the Officers are so pleased, and use no more delays.

The 8th of August [*N.S.*], the Officers of the ships took counsel together, with the Governor of the island, what they were best to do; thinking it not good to follow the King's advice; considering their long staying, and fearing some other hard fortune, if they should stay.

And because a great Galleon, being a Man of war and very strong, lay then before the island, wherein was the Governor of Brazil; which through foul weather, had put in there; they concluded that this Galleon, being well appointed, should sail with them to Lisbon. And although they did it, without the advice and commandment of the King; yet they had rather so adventure their lives upon the seas, than again to stay the danger of the haven. For that the winter did daily more and more increase; so that they were not to look for any better weather.

And, in that sort, appointing themselves as well as they could, and taking in all necessary provisions, the same day [30*th July, O.S.*], they all set sail, with no small fear of falling into some misfortune by the way.

But, because many that were of the ship of Malacca, stayed at Terceira to save such goods as, by any means, might be saved; and by that means to help themselves: among the which was the Factor of the Pepper, being one of my acquaintance. At whose request, as also because the pepper of that ship, and of all the other ships belonged all to one Farmer, by whom I was appointed Factor; seeing the necessity he had, and that he alone could hardly despatch so great a matter: I took order for mine own affairs [*charge*], and, having despatched it by other ships; I stayed there to help him, till we had further advice and orders from the Farmers of the pepper and other spices and wares. Of the which goods, we saved a great quantity by means of duckers [*divers*] and instruments that we used: having advices from the Farmers and the King, that it should not be long before they sent for us, willing us to stay there and to look unto the goods.

This staying and fetching us away, continued, as I said before, for the space of two years and a half; whereby you may consider the good order and policy of the Admiralty of Portugal, and with what diligence and care they seek for the common profit of the land, and the poor Merchants of the country: whom they ought to favour and help as much as they possibly may; but they do clean contrary, as those which deal in Portugal do well find.

The [3*rd O. S.*] 13th [*N. S.*] of August, the ships came back again to the island of Terceira, because they had a contrary wind, as also for want of fresh water: but they anchored not.

The day before [*i.e., 2nd of August, O. S., see pp.* 93, 188], the Earl of CUMBERLAND, with six or seven ships of war, sailed by the island of Terceira; and to their good fortune, passed out of sight: so that they despatched themselves in all haste;

and, for the more security, took with them 400 Spaniards of those that lay in the garrison in the island.

With them, they sailed towards Lisbon, having a good wind; so that within an eleven days after, they arrived in the river of Lisbon, with great gladness and triumph. For if they had stayed but one day longer before they had entered the river, they had all been taken by Sir FRANCIS DRAKE; who, with forty ships came before Cascaes, at the same time that the Indian ships cast anchor in the river of Lisbon; being guarded thither by divers galleys.

Now, by the discourse of this long and perilous voyage [*which as regards the* Santa Cruz, *the quickest of the five Carracks, lasted from 20th January to the 24th August* 1589 *N.S.*, 217 *days; against the smoother voyage outward, in* 1583, *of the* San Salvador, *in* 166 *days, see pp.* 19, 20], you may sufficiently perceive how that only, by the grace and special favour of GOD, the Indian ships do perform their voyages; yet with great misery, pain, labour, loss, and hindrance; whereby man may likewise consider the manner of their navigation, ordinances, customs, and governments of their ships. So that in comparison of many other voyages, this present voyage may be esteemed a happy and prosperous one. For oftentimes it chanceth that but one or two, of the five that yearly sail to India come safe home; as of late it hath been seen: some being taken, and some lost altogether by their own follies and bad order.

The Azores.

THEY are called *Azores*, that is to say, "Spar-hawks," or "Hawks," because that, in their first discovery, they found many Sparhawks in them, whereof they hold the name: although at this day, there are not any to be found. They are also called the Flemish Islands, *i.e.*, of the Netherlanders: because the first that inhabited the same were Netherlanders; whereof, till this time, there is a great number of their offspring remaining, that, in manner and behaviour, are altogether like Netherlanders.

The principal island of them all, is that of Terceira, called *Insula de Jesus Christ de Terceira.* It is between fifteen or sixteen miles in compass; and is altogether a great cliff of land, whereby there is little room in it. For it is, as it were, walled round about with cliffs; but where any strand or sand is, there standeth a fort. It hath no havens, nor entrance of waters, for the security and safety of the ships; except that before the chief town, called Angra: where it hath an open haven which, in form, is like a Half Moon, by the Portuguese called *Angra;* whereof the town hath its name. It hath on the one side, in the manner of an elbow sticking forth, two high hills, called Bresil, which stretch into the sea; so that, afar off, they seem to be divided from the island. These hills are very high; so that a man, being upon them, in clear weather, may see at the least ten, twelve, and sometimes fifteen miles into the sea.

Upon these hills, there stand two small stone pillars, where there is a sentinel placed, that continually watcheth to see what ships are at sea; and so to advertise those of the island.

For as many ships as he seeth coming out of the West, that is, from the Spanish Indies [*Central America and the West Indies*] or Brazil, Cape de Verde, Guinea, and the Portuguese Indies, and all other ways lying south or west; for every ship, he setteth a flag upon the pillar in the west. And when the ships, which he descrieth, are more than five, then he setteth up a great Ancient [*ensign*]; betokening a great fleet of ships.

The like he doth upon the other pillar, which standeth in the East, for such ships as come from Portugal or other places out of the east or north parts.

These pillars may be easily seen in all places of the town, by reason of the highness of the hills; so that there is not one ship or sail that is at sea that maketh towards the island, but it is presently [*at once*] known throughout all the town, and over all the island. For the watch is not holden only upon those two hills jutting into the sea, but also upon all corners, hills, and cliffs throughout the island; and as soon as they perceive any ships, the Governer and rulers are presently advertised thereof, that they may take such order therein, as need requireth.

Upon the furthest corner in the sea stands a fort, right against another fort that answereth it; so that those two forts do shut and defend the mouth or open haven of the town; and no ship can neither go in or come forth without the licence of two forts [*see Vol. I. p.* 271].

This town of Angra is not only the chief town of Terceira, but also of all towns within the islands thereabouts. Therein are resident, the Bishop, the Governor for the King, and the chief place of judgement or tribunal seat of all the islands of the Azores.

All the islands of the Azores are inhabited by the Portuguese; but since the troubles in Portugal [*i.e., since* 1580, *when* PHILIP *II. acceded to the Portuguese throne*], there have been divers Spanish soldiers sent thither, and a Spanish Governor, that keep all the forts and castles in their possession: although the Portuguese are put to no charges, nor yet hardly used by them. For the soldiers are rather kept short, so that no one dareth to go out of the town without a licence: and therefore men may quietly travel throughout the island, both day and night, without any trouble.

Likewise, the islanders will not suffer any stranger to travel to see the country: and this order was not brought up by the Spaniards, but by the Portuguese themselves before their troubles. For they would not permit it. And what is more, all strangers that came thither, were usually appointed a certain street, wherein they should sell their wares; and they might not go out of that street. Now, it is not so straitly looked unto, but they may go in all places of the town, and within the island: but not about it, to view the coast. Which, notwithstanding, was granted to us by the Governor himself, who lent us his horses to ride about; and gave us leave to see all the forts: which, at this time, is not permitted to the natural born islanders; neither are they so much credited.

We rode about the island twice, which he granted us leave to do, by means of a certain particular friendship we had with him: neither could the Portuguese hinder us therein, because we were in the King's service, as "Factors for the King's Pepper," and because they held and accounted us as natural born Portuguese. For the Governor would willingly have had me to have drawn a plot [*map*] of the whole island, that he might have sent it to the King: wherein I excused myself; yet I made him one of the town, with the haven, coming in, and forts of Angra, which he sent to the King: for which the Governor was greatly affected unto me, and showed me much friendship. We had, in our lodging, a French merchant, and a Scot, who willingly would have gone with us, to see the island; but could not be suffered: for the Portuguese think they would take the proportion thereof, and so seek to defeat [*wrest*] them of their right.

Such as are not merchants or workmen in the wood of the islands, wait for the fleets that come and go, to and from the Spanish and Portuguese Indies, Brazil, Cape de Verde, and Guinea, which do commonly come to Terceira to refresh themselves, as situated very fitly for that purpose. So that all the inhabitants do thereby richly maintain themselves, and sell all their wares, as well handiworks as victuals, to those ships: and all the islands roundabout do come to Terceira with their wares to sell them there. For the which cause, the Englishmen and other strangers keep continually about those islands; being assured that all ships, for want of refreshing, must of force, put into those islands: although, at this time [*i.e.*, 1594], many ships do avoid those islands, to the great discommodity both of the islands and the ships.

While I remained in Terceira, the Earl of CUMBERLAND came to Santa Maria (where there are no Spaniards, because it is a stout country like Terceira, and hard to board [*land on*]; whereby the inhabitants themselves are sufficient and able to defend it), to take in fresh water and some other victuals [*see p.* 199]; but the inhabitants would not suffer him to have it, and wounded divers of his men: whereby they were forced to depart, without having anything there.

About seven or eight miles north-north-west from Terceira, lieth the little island called Graciosa, which is but five and six miles in compass. A very pleasant, fine island, full of fruits and all other victuals; so that it not only feedeth itself, but also Terceira and the other islands about it; and hath no other kind of merchandise. It is well built, and inhabited by Portuguese; and hath no soldiers in it because it is not able to bear the charge.

The Earl of CUMBERLAND, while I lay in Terceira, came unto that island [*see pp.* 188-9]; where he in person, with seven or eight in his company, went on land; asking for certain beasts, hens, and other victuals, with wine and fresh water;

which they willingly gave him: and therewith he departed from thence, without doing them any hurt. For the which the inhabitants thanked him; and commended him for his courtesy, and keeping of his promise.

Fayal aboundeth in all sorts of victuals and fish; so that from this island, the most part of the victuals and necessaries come, by whole caravels, to Terceira. It hath likewise much woad, so that many English ships do traffic thither. The principal road and place, is the town of Villa Dorta. There the ships do likewise lie on the open sea under the land, as they do before all the other islands. By this town, there lieth a fortress, but it is of small importance.

And because the inhabitants, of themselves, did offer to defend the island against all enemies; the soldiers, which before that time lay in the fort, were discharged from thence: the islanders complaining that they were not able to maintain, nor lodge them.

The same time that the Earl of CUMBERLAND was in the island of Graciosa, he came likewise to Fayal [*see pp.* 190-4], where, at the first time, that he came, they began to resist him; but, by reason of some controversy between them, they let him land: where he razed the castle to the ground, and sank all their ordnance in the sea; taking with him, certain caravels and ships that lay in the road, with provisions of all things that he wanted, and therewith departed again to sea.

Whereupon, the King caused the principal actors therein to be punished; and sent out a company of [Spanish] soldiers; which went out of Terceira, with all kind of warlike munition and great shot: who made up the fortress again, the better to defend the island, trusting no more to the Portuguese.

In that island, are the most part of the Netherlanders' offspring; yet they use the Portuguese language, by reason they have been so long conversant among them; and those that used the Dutch tongue are all dead. They are great affected [*very kind*] to the Netherlanders and strangers.

Between Corvo and Flores [*70 miles west of Terceira*], and round about them, the Englishmen do commonly stay, to watch the ships that come out of the West: for those are the first islands that the ships look out for and descry, when they sail into Terceira.

Of certain notable and memorable incidents that happened during LINSCHOTEN's continuance in Terceira, from October 1589, to July 1592.

1589.

THE 2nd of October, *anno* 1589 [*N.S.*], at the town of Villa da Praya in the island of Terceira, two men being in a field hard without the town, were killed with lightning.

The 9th of the same month, there arrived in Terceira [*O.S.*, *see p.* 197] fourteen ships that came from the Spanish Indies, laden with cochineal, hides, gold, silver, pearls, and other rich wares. There were fifty in company when they departed out of Havanna: whereof, in their coming out of the Channel, eleven sank in the Channel by foul weather; and the rest, by a storm, were scattered and separated one from the other.

The next day [10*th*], there came another ship of the same company, that sailed close under the island so to get into the road: where she met with an English ship that had not above three cast pieces; and the Spaniard had twelve. They fought a long time together; which we, being in the island, might stand and behold. Whereupon the Governor of Terceira sent two boats of musketeers to help the ship: but before they could come to her, the English ship had shot her under water; and we saw her sink into the sea, with all her sails up, so that not anything was seen of her above the water.

The Englishmen, with their boat, saved the Captain and about thirty others with him; but not one pennyworth of the goods: and yet in the ship, there was, at the least, to the value of 200,000 ducats [=*about* £55,000 *then* = *about* £330,000 *now*] in gold, silver, and pearls. The rest of the men were drowned, which might be about fifty persons;

among the which were some friars and women, which the English would not save. Those that they did save, they set on land; and then they sailed away.

The [*17th O.S.*] 27th [*N.S.*] of the same month, the said fourteen ships, having refreshed themselves in the island, departed from Terceira towards Seville; and coming upon the coast of Spain, they were taken by the English ships that lay there to watch for them, two only excepted, which escaped away. The rest were wholly carried into England.

About the same time, the Earl of CUMBERLAND, with one of the Queen's ships, and five or six more, kept about those islands: and oftentimes came so close under the island and to the road of Angra, that the people on land might easily tell all his men that he had aboard, and knew such as walked on the hatches; they of the island not once shooting at them, although they might easily have done it, for they were within musket shot both of the town and fort.

In these places, he continued for the space of two months [*or rather, from 11th August to 10th November N.S.*], sailed round about the islands, and landed in Graciosa and Fayal, as in the descriptions of those islands [*pp.* 100-1] I have already declared. Here he took divers ships and caravels, which he sent into England: so that those of the island durst not once put forth their heads.

At the same time, about three or four days after the Earl of CUMBERLAND had been in the island of Fayal, and was departed thence [*which was on the 16th O.S., or 26th, N.S., September,* 1589 *pp.* 193-4], there arrived there six [West] Indian ships, whose General was one JUAN DORIVES, and there they discharged on that island 40,000,000 [*ducats = about* £10,000,000 (*ten millions sterling*) *then = about* £60,000,000 (*sixty millions sterling*) *now*] of gold and silver.

Having, with all speed, refreshed their ships; fearing the coming of the Englishmen, they set sail, and arrived safely in San Lucar de Barrameda, not meeting with the enemy; to the great good luck of the Spaniards, and hard fortune of the Englishmen. For that, within less than two days after the gold and silver were laden again into the Spanish ships, the Earl of CUMBERLAND sailed again by that island [*viz., on 23rd September, O.S., or 3rd October, N.S.,* 1589, *pp.* 194-7]. So that it appeared that GOD would not let them have it: for if they had once had sight thereof, without doubt it had been theirs; as the Spaniards themselves confessed.

In the month of November, there arrived in Terceira, two ships, which were the admiral and vice-admiral of the fleet, ladened with silver; who, with stormy weather, were separated from the fleet, and had been in great torment and distress, and ready to sink. For they were forced to use all their pumps, so that they wished, a thousand times, to have met with the Englishmen: to whom they would willingly have given their silver and all that ever they brought with them; only to save their lives. Although the Earl of CUMBERLAND lay still about those islands: yet they met not with him: so that, after much pain and labour, they got into the road before Angra: where, with all speed, they unladed and discharged above 5,000,000 of silver [*i.e., to the value of* 5,000,000 (*five millions*) *of ducats = about* £1,500,000 (*a million and a half sterling*) *then = about* £9,000,000 (*nine millions sterling*) *now*]; all in pieces of 8 lbs. to 10 lbs. weight. So that the whole quay lay covered with plates, and chests of silver full of Rials of Eight, most wonderful to behold. Each million being ten hundred thousand ducats; besides gold, pearls, and other precious stones, which were not registered.

The Admiral and Chief Commander of those ships and that fleet, called ALVARO FLORES DE QUINIONES, was sick of a disease (whereof, not long, after he died in Seville) was brought to land.

He brought with him the King's broad seal, and full authority to be General and Chief Commander upon the seas, and of all fleets and ships, and of all places, islands, or land wheresoever he came to. Whereupon, the Governor of Terceira did him great honour.

Between them, it was concluded that, perceiving the weakness of their ships, and the danger through the Englishmen, they would send the ships empty, with soldiers to convey them, either to Seville or Lisbon, whichever they could first arrive at, with advice to His Majesty of all that had passed; and that he would give order to fetch the silver with a good and safe convoy. Whereupon, the said ALVARO FLORES stayed there, under colour of keeping the silver; but specially because of his disease, and that they were afraid of the Englishmen. This ALVARO FLORES had alone, for his own part, above 50,000 ducats [= *about* £13,000 *then* = *about* £100,000 *now*] in pearls: which he shewed unto us, and sought to sell them; or barter them with us, for spices or bills of exchange.

The said two ships set sail, with 300 or 400 men, as well soldiers as others, that came with them out of [the West] India: and being at sea, had a storm, wherewith the admiral burst asunder, and sank in the sea; not one man saved. The vice-admiral cut down her mast, and ran the ship on ground hard by Setubal, where it burst in pieces: and some of the men, saving themselves by swimming, brought the news; the rest were drowned.

In the same month [*November* 1589], there came two great ships out of the Spanish Indies, that, within half a mile of the road of Terceira, met with an English ship; which, after they had fought long together, took them both.

[The following history of the English ship and her crew is very extraordinary.]

About seven or eight months before [*i.e., about April* 1589], there had been an English ship in Terceira, that, under the name of a Frenchman, came to traffic in the island, there to lade wood: and being discovered, both ship [*p.* 190] and goods were confiscated to the King's use; and all the men kept prisoners. Yet went they up and down the streets to get their living, by labouring like slaves; being indeed as safe in that island, as if they had been in prison.

But, in the end, upon a Sunday [31*st of August, O.S., see p.* 190; 10*th September, N.S.*], all the sailors went down behind the hills, called Bresil, where they found a fisher-boat; whereinto they got, and rowed into [*out to*] the sea, to the Earl of CUMBERLAND's ship, which, to their great fortune, chanced, at that time, to come by the island [*see p.* 190]; and who had anchored, with his ships, about half a mile from the road of Angra, hard by two small islands, which lie about a base's shot from the island, and are full of goats, bucks, and sheep, belonging to the inhabitants of Terceira. Those sailors knew it well, and thereupon they rowed unto them with their boats; and lying at anchor, that day, they fetched as many goats and sheep as they had need of: which those of the town and island saw well, yet durst not once go forth.

So there remained no more on land, but the Master, and

the Merchant [*Supercargo*] of the said English ship. This Master had a brother-in-law dwelling in England; who, having news of his brother's imprisonment in Terceira, got licence of the Queen of England to set forth a ship: therewith to see if he could recover his losses of the Spaniards, by taking some of them; and so to redeem his brother, that lay prisoner in Terceira. And he it was, that took the [above] two Spanish ships before the town [*in November* 1589]; the Master of the aforesaid ship, standing on the shore by me, and looking upon them; for he was my great acquaintance.

The ships being taken, that were worth 300,000 ducats [=£80,000 *then*=£480,000 *now*]; he sent all the men on land, saving only two of the principal gentlemen whom he kept aboard, thereby to ransom his brother: and sent the [Spanish] Pilot of one of the [two West] Indian ships that were taken, with a letter to the Governor of Terceira, wherein he wrote that "He should deliver him his brother, and he would send the two gentlemen on land. If not, he would sail with them into England." As indeed he did: because the Governor would not do it; saying that "The gentlemen might make that suit to the King of Spain himself."

This Spanish Pilot, and the English Master likewise, we bade to supper with us: where the Pilot shewed us all the manner of their fight; much commending the order and manner of the Englishmen's fighting, as also for their courteous using of him.

But, in the end, the English Master likewise stole away in a French ship, without paying any ransom as yet [*i.e., up to July* 1592].

1590.

In the month of January 1590, there arrived one ship alone [*by itself*] in Terceira, that came from the Spanish Indies; and brought the news that there was a fleet of a hundred ships, which put out from the Firm Land [*the Spanish Main, or Central America*] of the Spanish Indies: and by a storm, were driven upon the coast, called Florida; where they were all cast away, she having only escaped. Wherein there were great riches, and many men lost; as may well be thought.

So that they made their account, that of 220 ships that, for certain, were known to have put out of New Spain [*Mexico*]

Santo Domingo, Havana, Cape de Verde, Brazil, Guinea, &c., in the year 1589, to sail for Spain and Portugal: there were not above 14 or 15 of them, that arrived there in safety. All the rest, were either drowned, burst [*foundered*], or taken.

In the same month of January, there arrived in Terceira, 15 or 16 ships that came from Seville; which were mostly Fly-boats of the Low Countries, and some Breton ships, that were arrested in Spain. These came full of soldiers and well appointed with munition, by the King's commandment, to lade the silver that lay in Terceira; and to fetch ALVARO DE FLORES to Spain.

And because, at that time of the year, there are always storms about those islands, therefore they durst not enter into the road of Terceira. For as then it blew so great a storm, that some of their ships that had anchored, were forced to cut down their masts, and were in danger of being lost: and among the rest, a ship of Biscay ran against the land, and was stricken in pieces; but all the men saved themselves.

The other ships were forced to keep the sea, and separated themselves the one from the other, where wind and weather would drive them, until the 15th of March [1590]. For that, in all that time, they could not have one day of fair weather to anchor in: whereby they endured much misery; cursing both the silver and the island.

This storm being passed; they chanced to meet with a small English ship, of about 40 tons in bigness, which, by reason of the great wind, could not bear all her sails; so they set upon her and took her: and with the English flag in their admiral's [*flag ship's*] stern, they came as proudly into the haven, as if they had conquered all the realm of England. But as the admiral, that bare the English flag upon her stern, was entering into the road; there came, by chance, two English ships by the island that paid her so well for her pains, that they were forced to cry *Misericordia!* and without all doubt, had taken her, if she had been a mile further in the [*out at*] sea. But because she got under the fortress, which also began to shoot at the Englishmen, they were forced to leave her, and to put further into the sea; having slain five or six of the Spaniards.

The Englishmen that were taken in the small ship, were put under hatches, and coupled in bolts. After they had been prisoners three or four days [*i.e., about* 18*th of March* 1590 *N.S.*], there was a Spanish Ensign-bearer in the ship, that had a brother slain in the fleet that came for England [*the Armada of* 1588], who (then minding to revenge his death, and withal to shew his manhood to the English captives that were in the English ship, which they had taken as is aforesaid) took a poinard in his hand, and went down under the hatches; where, finding the poor Englishmen sitting in bolts; with the same poinard he stabbed six of them to the heart: which two others of them perceiving, clasped each other about the middle because they would not be murdered by him, and threw themselves into the sea, and there were drowned.

This act was much disliked and very ill taken of all the Spaniards; so they carried the Spaniard a prisoner unto Lisbon: where, being arrived, the King of Spain willed that he should be sent to England, that the Queen of England might use him as she thought good; which sentence, his friends got reversed. Notwithstanding he commanded that he should, without all favour, be beheaded: but upon a Good Friday [? *in* 1590 *or* 1591], the Cardinal going to *Mass*; all the Captains and Commanders made so great entreaty for him, that, in the end, they got his pardon.

This I thought good to note, that men may understand the bloody and dishonest minds of the Spaniards, when they have men under their subjection.

The same two English ships which followed the Spanish Admiral till he had got under the fort of Terceira, as I said before, put into the [*out to*] sea; where they met with another Spanish ship, being of the same fleet, that had likewise been scattered by the storm, and was [the] only [one] missing, for the rest lay in the road.

This small ship the Englishmen took, and sent all the men on shore, not hurting any of them; but if they had known what had been done unto the aforesaid English captives, I believe they would soon have revenged themselves: as, afterwards, many innocent soul paid for it.

This ship, thus taken by the Englishmen, was the same that was kept and confiscated in the island of Terceira; the Englishmen of which got out of the island in a fisher-boat, as I said before [*p.* 105]; and was sold to the Spaniards that then came from the [West] Indies [*p.* 103]; wherewith they sailed to San Lucar de Barrameda: where it was also arrested by the Duke, and appointed to go in the company to fetch the silver in Terceira, because it was the ship that sailed well; but among the Spaniards' fleet, it was the meanest of the company. By this means, it was taken from the Spaniards and carried into England; and the owners had it again, when they least thought of it.

The 19th of March, the aforesaid ships, being nineteen in number, having laden the King's silver, and received ALVARO FLORES DE QUINIONES with his company, and a good provision of necessaries and munition; and of soldiers that were fully resolved, as they made shew, to fight valiantly to the last man, before they would yield or lose their riches.

Although they set their course for San Lucar, the wind drave them to Lisbon. Which, as it seemed, was willing by his force to help them, and to bring them thither in safety: although ALVARO DE FLORES, both against the wind and weather, would, perforce, have sailed to San Lucar; but being constrained by the wind, and the importunity of the sailors (who *protested* they would require their losses and damages of him), he was content to sail to Lisbon. From whence, the silver was carried by land to Seville.

At Cape St. Vincent, there lay a fleet of twenty English ships, to watch for this *armada*; so that if they had put into San Lucar, they had fallen right into their hands: which if the wind had served, they had done. And, therefore, they may say that the wind had lent them a happy voyage.

For if the Englishmen had met with them, they had surely been in great danger; and possibly but few of them had escaped, by reason of the fear wherewith they were possessed that "Fortune, or rather, GOD was wholly against them." Which is a sufficient cause, to make the Spaniards out of heart; and, on the contrary, to give the Englishmen more courage, and to make them bolder. For they are victorious, stout, and valiant; and all their enterprises do take so good effect, that they are, thereby, become Lords and Masters of the Sea, and need care for no man: as it well appeareth, by this brief Discourse.

In the month of March 1590, there was a blazing star [*a Comet*] with a tail, seen in Terceira, that continued four nights together, stretching the tail towards the south.

In the month of May, a caravel of Fayal arrived in the haven or road of Angra, at Terceira, ladened with oxen, sheep, hens, and other kinds of victuals; and full of people She had, by a storm, broken her rudder; whereby the sea cast her about, and there she sank. In her, were drowned three children and a Franciscan friar. The rest of the men saved themselves by swimming, and by help from the shore; but the cattle and hens came drowned to land.

The friar was buried with a great procession and solemnity; being esteemed a saint, because he was taken up dead with his book between his arms: for the which cause, every man came to look on him as a miracle, giving great offerings, to say *masses* for his soul.

[What now follows is an enormous falsehood, being apparently only an exaggerated rumour of CAVENDISH's Expedition to the South Seas, 21st July, 1586—10 September 1588.

The 1st of August [1590] the Governor of Terceira received advices out of Portugal and Spain, that two years before the date of his letters [*i.e.*, *in* 1588], there sailed out of England twelve great well-appointed ships; with full resolution to take their journey, seven of them to the Portuguese Indies, and the other five to Malacca. Of which, five were cast away in the Straits of Magellan, and three sailed to Malacca: but what they had done there, was as then not known.

[LINSCHOTEN's friend AFHUISEN, who left Malacca, at a much later date, *viz.*, about December 1588, *p.* 118, was then at Angra; and would, of course, be able to contradict this part of this immense offspring of fear.]

The other seven passed the Cape of Good Hope, and arrived in India, whither they put in at the coast of Malabar, and there took six foists of the Malabars, but let them go again; and [? *where*], two Turkish galleys that came out of the Straits of Mecca or Red Sea, to whom likewise they did no hurt. And there [? *where*], they laded their ships with spices, and returned back again on their way: but where, or in what place they had ladened, it was not certainly known[!]. Saving only, that this much was written by the Governor of India; and sent over land to Venice, and from thence to Madrid.

The 7th of August, a navy of English ships was seen before Terceira, being twenty in number, and five of them Queen's ships. Their General was one Sir MARTIN FROBISHER; as we, after, had intelligence. They came purposely to watch for the Fleet of the Spanish Indies, for the [Portuguese] Indian ships, and for the ships of the countries in the West.

Which put the islanders in great fear, specially those of Fayal. For the Englishmen had sent a Trumpeter to the Governer there, to ask for certain wine, flesh, and other victuals, for their money and good friendship. They of Fayal, did not only refuse to give ear to them; but with a shot, killed their messenger or trumpeter: which the English took in evil part, sending them word that "They were best to look to themselves, and stand upon their guard; for they meant to come and visit them, whether they would or not." The Governor there made them answer, that "He was there on the behalf of His Majesty of Spain; and that he would do his best to keep them out." But nothing was done: although they of Fayal were in no little fear; sending to Terceira for aid: from whence, they had certain barks with powder and munition for war, together with some biscuit and other necessary provision.

The 30th of August, we received very certain news out of Portugal, that there were eighty ships put out of the Corunna [*called by the English, the Groine*], laden with victuals, munition, money, and soldiers, to go for Brittany; to aid the Catholics and Leaguers of France against the King of Navarre.

At the same time, two Netherland Hulks coming out of Portugal to Terceira, being half over the seas, met with four of the Queen's ships, their General being Sir JOHN HAWKINS, that stayed them; but let them go again, without doing them any harm.

The Netherlanders reported that "Each of the Queen's ships had eighty pieces of ordnance; that Sir FRANCIS DRAKE lay with forty ships in the English Channel watching for the *armada* from the Corunna; and that likewise, there lay at Cape St. Vincent ten other English ship, that if any of the ships escaped from the Islands [*i.e., the Azores*] they might take them."

This tidings put the islanders in great fear; lest if they

failed of the Spanish fleet, and got nothing by them, they would then fall upon the Islands, as they would not return empty: whereupon they held straight watch, sending advices to the King, of the news they had heard.

The 1st of September, there came to the island of St. Michael, a Portuguese ship out of the haven of Pernambuco in Brazil, which brought news that the Admiral of the Portuguese fleet that came from India, having missed the island of St. Helena, was, of necessity, constrained to put into Pernambuco: although the King had expressly, under a great penalty, forbidden him so to do; because of the worms, that do there spoil the ships.

The same ship, wherein BERNADINE RIBERO was Admiral, the year before [1589], sailed out of Lisbon to the Indies, with five ships in her company; whereof but four got to India; the fifth was never heard of, so that it was thought to be cast away. The other four returned safe again to Portugal [this year 1590]: though the admiral was much spoiled, because he met with two English ships that fought long with him, and slew many of his men; but yet he escaped from them.

The 5th of the same month, there arrived at Terceira, a caravel of the island of Corvo, and brought with her 50 men that had been spoiled by the Englishmen, who had set them on shore in the island of Corvo; having taken them out of a ship that came from the Spanish Indies.

They brought tidings that "The Englishmen had taken four more of the [West] Indian ships, and a Caravel of Advices with the King of Spain's Letters of Advices for the ships [*Carracks*] coming out of the Portugal Indies. And that, with those which they had taken, there were at the least forty English ships together; so that not one bark escaped them, but fell into their hands."

Therefore the Portuguese ships coming out of India durst not put into the Islands; but took their course under 40° N., and 42° N., and from thence sailed to Lisbon; shunning likewise the Cape St. Vincent: otherwise they could not have had a prosperous journey of it; for that then, the sea was full of English ships.

Whereupon, the King advised the fleet lying at Havanna in the Spanish Indies, ready to come for Spain, that they should stay there all that year, till the next year; because of the great danger they might fall into by the Englishmen.

Which was no small charge and hindrance to the fleet, for the ships that lie there, do consume themselves, and in a manner eat up one another; by reason of the great number of people, together with the scarcity of all things. So that many ships chose rather, one by one, to adventure themselves alone, to get home than to stay there. All which fell into the Englishmen's hands; the men of divers of which, were brought to Terceira. For, for a whole day, we could see nothing else but spoiled men set on shore, some out of one ship, some out of another, that it was a pity to see all of them cursing the English and their own fortunes; with those that had been the causes to provoke the Englishmen to fight: and complaining of the small remedy and order taken therein by the King of Spain's Officers.

The 19th of the same month, there came a caravel of Lisbon to Terceira, with one of the King's Officers, to cause the goods that were saved out of the ship that came from Malacca (for the which, we stayed there) to be ladened and sent to Lisbon.

At the same time, there put out of the Corunna, one Don ALONSO DE BASSAN, with 40 great Ships of war, to come to the islands [of the Azores], there to watch for the fleets of the Spanish and Portuguese Indies: and the goods of the Malacca ship being ladened, they were to convoy them all together to the river of Lisbon. But being certain days at sea, always with a contrary wind, they could not get unto the Islands. Only two of them, scattered from the fleet, arrived at Terceira; and, not finding the fleet, they presently returned back to seek them.

In the meantime, the King changed his mind, and caused the fleet to stay in [West] India, as I said before; and therefore he sent word unto Don ALONSO DE BASSAN that he should return again to Corunna, which he presently did: without doing anything, or once approaching near the islands, saving only the two foresaid ships. For he well knew that the Englishmen lay by the island of Corvo; but he would not visit them. So he returned to the haven of Corunna; whereby our goods that come from Malacca were yet to ship; and being trussed up again, we were forced to stay a more fortunate time, with patience.

The 23rd of October, there arrived at Terceira, a caravel with advices out of Portugal, that of the five ships which [about April] in the year 1590, were laden in Lisbon, for the the [East] Indies, four of them were turned back again to Portugal, after they had been four months abroad: and that the admiral, wherein the Viceroy, called MATTHIAS D'ALBUQUERQUE, sailed, had only got to India: as afterward news thereof was brought overland; having been, at the least, eleven months at sea and never saw land, and came in great misery to Malacca.

In this ship there died by the way, 280 men, according to a note, made by himself and sent to the Cardinal of Lisbon, with the name and surname of every man; together with a description of his voyage and the misery they had endured: which was only done because he would not lose the Government of India; and for that cause, he had sworn either to lose his life, or to arrive in India. As, indeed, he did afterwards: but to the great danger, loss, and hinderance of his company, that were forced to buy it with their lives; and only for want of provisions, as it may well be thought. For he knew full well, that if he had returned back again to Portugal, as the other ships did, he should have been cashiered from his Indian Regiment; because the people began already to murmur at him for his proud and lofty mind.

And among other things, that which shewed his pride the more, he caused to be painted above the gallery of his ship, Fortune, and his own picture with a staff standing by her, as it were, threatening her, with this posy, *Queroque vencas!* that is, "I will have thee to overcome!" which being read by the Cardinal and other gentlemen, that, to honour him, brought him aboard his ship; it was thought to be a point of exceeding folly.

But it is no strange matter among the Portuguese: for they, above all others, must, of force, let the fool peep out of their sleeves; specially when they are in authority. For I knew the said MATTHIAS D'ALBUQUERQUE in India, being a soldier and a Captain; where he was esteemed and accounted for one of the best of them: and much honoured and beloved of all men, as behaving himself courteously to every man; whereby they all desired that he might be Viceroy. But when he had once received his *Patent*, with full power and authority from the

King to be Viceroy; he changed so much from his former behaviour, that by reason of his pride, they all began to fear and curse him; and that, before he departed out of Lisbon: as is often seen in many men, that are advanced into State and dignity.

1591.

The 20th of January, *anno* 1591, there was news brought out of Portugal to Terceira, that the Englishmen had taken a ship that the King had sent to the Portuguese Indies, with advices to the Viceroy, of the returning again of the four ships that should have gone to India. And because those ships were come back again, that ship was stuffed and ladened, as full of goods as it possibly might be; having likewise, in ready money, 500,000 ducats [=*about* £137,500 *then*=£825,000 *now*] in Rials of Eight; besides other wares.

It departed from Lisbon in the month of November 1590, and met with the Englishmen; with whom, for a time, it fought: but, in the end, it was taken and carried into England, with men and all. Yet when they came there, the men were set at liberty; and returned to Lisbon, where the Captain was committed a prisoner; but he excused himself, and was released. With whom, I spake myself; and he made this report to me.

At the same time also, they took a ship that came from the Mine [possibly *Sofala*, *see p.* 17]: and two ships, ladened with pepper and spices, that were to sail into Italy; the pepper alone that was in them being worth 170,000 ducats [= *about* £46,750 *then* = £280,000 *now*]. All these ships were carried into England, and made good prize.

In the month of July, *anno* 1591, there happened an earthquake in the island of St. Michael; which continued [*i.e., at intervals*] from the 26th of July to the 12th of August. In which time, no man durst stay within his house: but fled into the fields, fasting and praying; with great sorrow, because many of their houses fell down. A town, called Villa Franca, was almost clean razed to the ground; all the cloisters and houses shaken to the earth, and some people therein slain. In some places, the land rose up, and the cliffs removed from one place to another; and some hills were defaced, and made even with the ground. The earthquake was so strong, that the ships which lay in the road and on the sea, shaked as if the world would have turned round. There also sprang a fountain out of the earth; from whence, for the space of four days, there flowed a most clear water; and, after that, it ceased. At the same time, they heard such thunder and noise under the earth, as if all the devils in hell had been assembled in that place; wherewith many died for fear.

The island of Terceira shook four times together, so that it seemed to turn about: but there happened no misfortune unto it.

Earthquakes are common in these islands. For, about twenty years past, there happened another earthquake: wherein the half of a high hill, that lieth by the same town of Villa Franca, fell down, and covered all the town with earth; and killed many men.

The 25th of August, the King's *Armada*, coming out of Ferrol, arrived at Terceira, being in all thirty ships, Biscayens, Portuguese, and Spaniards; and ten Dutch Fly-boats that were arrested in Lisbon to serve the King: besides other small vessels, *pataxos* that came to serve as messengers from place to place, and to discover [*scout on*] the seas.

The Navy came to stay for, and convoy the ships that should come from the Spanish Indies; and the Fly-boats were appointed, in their turn, to take in the goods that were saved in the lost ship that came from Malacca, and to convey it to Lisbon.

The 13th of September, the said *Armada* arrived at the island of Corvo, where the Englishmen, with about sixteen ships, then lay, staying for the Spanish [West Indian] fleet; whereof some, or the most part were come, and there the English were in good hopes to have taken them.

But when they perceived the King's Army to be strong: the Admiral, being the Lord THOMAS HOWARD, commanded his fleet not to fall upon them; nor any of them once to separate their ships from him, unless he gave commission so to do.

Notwithstanding, the Vice-Admiral, Sir RICHARD GRENVILLE, being in the ship called the *Revenge* [*of* 700 *tons*], went into the Spanish fleet and shot among them, doing them great hurt; and thinking the rest of the company would have followed: which they did not, but left him there and sailed away. The cause why, could not be known. Which the Spaniards perceiving, with seven or eight ships they boarded her: but she withstood them all, fighting with them, at the least, twelve hours together: and sank two of them, one being a new Double Fly-boat, of 1,200 tons; the other, a Biscayen. But, in the end, by reason of the number that came upon her, she was taken; but their great loss: for they had lost in fighting and by drowning, above four hundred men. Of the Englishmen, there were slain about a hundred; Sir RICHARD GRENVILLE himself being wounded in the brain, whereof he died.

He was borne into the ship called the *San Paulo*, wherein was the Admiral of the fleet, Don ALONSO DE BASSAN. There, his wounds were dressed by the Spanish surgeons; but Don ALONSO himself would neither see him, nor speak with him. All the rest of the Captains and gentlemen went to visit him, and to comfort him in his hard fortune; wondering at his courage and stout heart, for he showed not any sign of faintness, nor changing of colour: but feeling the hour of death to approach, he spake these words in Spanish, and said, *Here die I, RICHARD GRENVILLE, with a joyful and quiet mind, for I have ended my life as a true soldier ought to do, that hath fought for his country, Queen, religion, and honour: whereby my soul most joyfully departeth out of this body; and shall leave behind it, an everlasting fame of* a valiant and true soldier, that hath done his duty, *as he was bound to do.* [*see p.* 126].

When he had finished these, or such like words, he gave up the ghost, with great and stout courage; and no man could perceive any true sign of heaviness in him.

This Sir RICHARD GRENVILLE was a great and rich gentleman in England, and had great yearly revenues, of his own inheritance: but he was a man very unquiet in his mind, and greatly affected to war, inasmuch, as of his own private motion, he offered his services to the Queen. He had performed many valiant acts, and was greatly feared in these islands [*see p.* 122], and known of every man: but of nature very severe, so that his own people hated him for his fierceness, and spake very hardly of him.

For when they first entered into the Fleet or *Armada*, they had their great sail in a readiness, and might, possibly enough, have sailed away; for it was one of the best ships for sailing in England. The Master perceiving that the other ships had left them, and followed not after; commanded the great sail to be cut, that they might make away: but Sir RICHARD GRENVILLE threatened both him and all the rest that were in the ship, that if any man laid hand upon it, he would cause him to be hanged. So by that occasion, they were compelled to fight; and, in the end, were taken.

He was of so hard a complexion that, as he continued among the Spanish Captains, while they were at dinner or supper with him, he was carouse three or four glasses of wine; and, in a bravery, take [successively] the glasses between his teeth, and crush them in pieces, and swallow them down, so that oftentimes the blood ran out of his mouth, without any harm at all to him: and this was told me, by divers credible persons that, many times, stood and beheld him.

The Englishmen that were left in the ship, as the Captain of the Soldiers, the Master, and others, were dispersed into divers of the Spanish ships that had taken them: where there had almost arisen a new fight between the Biscayens and the Portuguese: which each of them would have the honour to have first boarded her. So there grew a great noise and quarrel among them, one taking the chief ancient [*ensign*], and the other the flag: and the Captain and every one held his own.

The ships that had boarded her, were altogether out of order and broken; and many of their men hurt: whereby they were compelled to come to the island of Terceira, there to repair themselves. Where, being arrived, I and my chamber-fellow [*i.e.*, *AFHUISEN*], to hear some news, went on board one of the ships, being a great Biscayen, and one of the *twelve Apostles*, whose Captain was called BARTANDONO, that had been General of the Biscayens in the Fleet that went for England [*i.e., the Spanish Armada of* 1588]. He, seeing us, called us up into the gallery; where with great courtesy, he received us: being then set at dinner with the English Captain [*i.e.*, of the Soldiers of the *Revenge*], that sate by him, and had on a suit of black velvet; but he could not tell us anything, for he could speak no other language but English, and Latin, which BARTANDONO could also speak a little.

The English Captain got licence of the Governor, that he might come on land, with his weapon by his side; and was in our lodging, with the Englishman [*i.e., the Merchant or Supercargo, mentioned on p.* 106] that was kept prisoner in the island (being of that ship whereof the sailors got away, as I said before). The Governor of Terceira bade him to dinner; and shewed him great courtesy.

The Master likewise, with licence of BARTANDONO, came on shore, and was in our lodging. He had, at the least, ten or twelve wounds, as well in his head as on his body: whereof, after, being at sea between the Islands and Lisbon, he died.

The Captain wrote a letter, wherein he declared all the manner of the fight; and left it with the English Merchant [*or Supercargo*] that lay in our lodging, to send it to the Lord Admiral of England.

This English Captain coming to Lisbon, was there well received, and not any hurt done unto him: but, with good convoy, sent to Setubal: and, from thence, with all the rest of the Englishmen that were taken prisoners, sailed into England.

The Spanish *Armada* stayed at the island of Corvo till the last of September, to assemble the rest of the fleet together; which, in the end, were to the number of 140 sail of ships, partly coming from [the West] India, and partly of the *Armada*. And being all together, ready to sail to Terceira, in good company; there suddenly rose so hard and cruel a storm that those of the island do affirm that, in man's memory, there was not any such seen or heard of before: for it seemed [as if] the sea would have swallowed up the Islands. The water mounted higher than the cliffs, which are so high that it amazeth a man to behold them; but the sea reached above them, and living fishes were thrown upon the land.

This storm continued not a day or two only, with one wind; but seven or eight days continually, the wind turning round about in all places of the compass, at the least, twice or thrice during that time: and all alike with a continual storm and tempest; most terrible to behold, even to us that were on shore, much more then to such as were at sea. So that on the coasts and cliffs of the island of Terceira alone, there were about twelve ships cast away; and that, not upon one side only, but round about it in every corner: whereby, nothing else was heard but complaining, crying, lamenting, and telling, "Here is a ship broken in pieces against the cliffs!" and "There, another! and the men drowned." So that, for the space of twenty days after the storm, they did nothing else but fish for dead men, that continually came driving on the shore.

Among the rest, was the English ship called the *Revenge*, that was cast away upon a cliff, near to the island of Terceira; where it break into a hundred pieces, and sank to the ground: having in her, seventy men, Gallicians, Biscayens, and others, with some of the captive Englishmen; whereof but one was saved, that got up upon the cliffs alive, and had his body and head all wounded. He, being on shore, brought us the news, desiring to be shriven; and thereupon presently died. The *Revenge* had in her, divers fair brass pieces, that were all sunk in the sea; which they of the island were in good hope to weigh up again.

The next summer after [*i.e.*, 1592], among these ships, that were cast away about Terceira, was likewise a Fly-boat called the *White Dove* (being one of those that had been arrested in Portugal to serve the King), lost there. The Master of her, was one CORNELIUS MARTENSON, of Schiedam in Holland; and there were in her, as in every one of the rest, one hundred soldiers. He, being overruled by their Captain, that he could not be master of his own, sailing here and there at the mercy of GOD, as the storm drove him; in the end, came within sight of the island of Terceira. Which the Spaniards perceiving, thought all their safety only to consist in putting into the road; compelling the Master and Pilot to make towards the island. The Master refused to do it, saying, that "They were most sure there to be cast away, and utterly spoiled": but the Captain called him, "Drunkard! and Heretic!" and striking him with a staff, commanded him to do as he would have him.

The Master seeing this, and being compelled to do it, said, "Well, my masters! seeing it is the desire of you all to be cast away! I can but lose one life!" and therewith desperately, he sailed towards the shore; and was on that side of the island where there was nothing else but hard stones, and rocks as high as mountains, most terrible to behold: where some of the inhabitants stood, with long ropes and corks bound at the end thereof, to throw them down to the men that they might lay hold upon them and save their lives; but few of them got so near, most of them been cast away, and smitten in pieces, before they could get to the wall.

The ship sailing in this manner towards the island, and approaching to the shore; the Master (being an old man and full of years) called his son, that was in the ship with him, and having embraced one another, and taken their last farewell, the good old father willed his son not to take care for him, but to seek to save himself: "For" said he, "son! thou art young: and may have some hope to save thy life; but as for me, I am old, it is no great matter what becomes of me." Therewith, each of these, shedding many tears (as every loving father and kind child may well consider) the ship fell upon the cliffs, and brake in pieces: the father falling into the sea, on the one side, and the son on the other; each laying hold on that which came next to hand, but to no purpose. For the sea was so high and furious, that they were all drowned, but fourteen or fifteen who saved themselves by swimming, but yet with their legs and arms half broken and out of joint; among the which, were the Master's son, and four other Dutch boys. The rest of the Spaniards and sailors, with the Captain and Master, were drowned.

Whose heart would not melt with, to behold so grievous a sight? especially considering with himself, that the greatest cause thereof was the beastliness and insolency of the Spaniards; as in this only [*single*] example may well be seen.

Whereby may be considered how the other ships sped [*in the previous storm of October* 1591]: as we ourselves did in part behold, and by the men that were saved, did hear more at large; as also some others of our countrymen [*i.e., Dutchmen*] that, then, were in the like danger can well witness.

At the other islands, the loss [*in October* 1591] was no less than in Terceira. For on the island of St. George, there were two ships cast away; on the island of Pico, two ships; on the island of Graciosa, three ships: and besides those, there came everywhere round about, divers pieces of broken ships and other things, fleeting towards the islands; wherewith the sea was all covered, most pitiful to behold.

On the island of St. Michael, there were four ships cast away; and between Terceira and St. Michael, three more were sunk, which were seen, and heard to cry out: whereof not one man was saved. The rest put into the [*out to*] sea, without masts, all torn and rent.

So that of the whole fleet and *armada*, being 140 ships in all, there were but 32 or 33 arrived in Spain and Portugal: yea, and those few with so great misery, pain, and labour that no two of them arrived together; but this day one, and to-morrow another, the next day a third, and so on, one after the other, to the number aforesaid.

All the rest were cast away upon the Islands [*Azores*] and overwhelmed in the sea: whereby may be considered what great loss and hindrance they received at that time. For, by many men's judgements, it was esteemed to be much more than was left by the Army that came for England [*in* 1588]; and it may be well thought and presumed that it was no other but a just plague, purposely sent by GOD upon the Spaniards: and that it might truly be said, the taking of the *Revenge* was justly revenged upon them; and that, not by the might or force of man, but by the power of GOD.

As some of them openly said, in the isle of Terceira, that "They believed, verily, GOD would consume them; and that He took part with Lutherans and heretics." Saying further that "So soon as they had thrown the dead body of the Vice-admiral Sir RICHARD GRENVILLE overboard; they verily thought that, as he had a devilish faith and religion, and therefore that the devils loved him: so he presently sank down into the bottom of the sea, and down into hell, where he raised up all the devils to revenge his death; and that they brought so great storms and torments upon the Spaniards, only [*simply*] because they maintained the Catholic and Romish religion." Such, and such like blasphemies against GOD, they ceased not openly to utter; without any man reproving them nor their false opinions thereon: but the most part of them the rather said, and affirmed that "of truth, it must needs be so."

As one of these Indian fleets put out of New Spain, there were 35 of them, by storm and tempest, cast away and drowned in the sea: so that, out of 50 in all, but 15 escaped.

Of the fleet that came from Santo Domingo, there were 14

cast away, coming out of the Channel of Havanna; whereof the Admiral and Vice-admiral were two. From *Terra firma* in India [*i.e.*, *Central America*], there came two ships ladened with gold and silver; that were taken by the Englishmen. And before the Spanish *Armada* came to Corvo, the Englishmen, at different times, had taken, at the least, 20 ships, that came from Santo Domingo, [West] India, Brazil, &c.; and sent them all to England.

Whereby it plainly appeareth, that, in the end, GOD will assuredly plague the Spaniards: having already blinded them, so that they have not the sense to perceive it, but still to remain in their obstinate opinions. But it is lost labour to strive against GOD, and to trust in man; as being foundations erected upon the sands, which, with the wind, are blown down and overthrown : as we daily see before our eyes, and, not long since, have evidently observed in many places.

Therefore, let every man but look to his own actions! and take our Low Countries for an example: wherein, we can but blame our own sins and wickedness; which doth so blind us, that we wholly forget and reject the benefits of GOD, continuing the servants and yoke slaves of Satan. GOD, of His mercy! open our eyes and hearts! that we may know our only Health and Saviour, JESUS CHRIST; who only can help, govern, and preserve us; and give us a happy end in all our affairs.

LINSCHOTEN'S return home to Enkhuisen.

BY THE destruction of the Spaniards, and their evil success, the lading and shipping of the goods that were saved out of the ship that came from Malacca to Terceira, was again put off: and therefore we must have patience till it please GOD to send a fitter time; and that we received further advices and order from His Majesty of Spain.

All this being thus past, the Farmers and other merchants (seeing that the hope of any *armada* or ships in the King's behalf to be sent to fetch the goods, was all in vain) made request unto His Majesty that he would grant them licence, for every man particularly [*individually*] to ship his goods in what ship he would, at his own adventure; which, after long suit, was granted in the end: upon condition that every man should put in sureties to deliver the goods into the Custom House at Lisbon, to the end that the King might be paid his custom; as also that the goods, delivered to them in Terceira, should all be registered.

Whereupon, the Farmers of Pepper, with other merchants, agreed with a Flushinger, to fetch all the cloves, nutmegs, mace, and other, spices, and goods that belonged to them; excepting only the pepper, which the King as then would not grant to lade.

The same ship arrived at Terceira, about the last of November; and, because it was somewhat dangerous, being the latter end of the year, we laded her with all the speed we could: for then the coast was clear of Englishmen.

To be short. This Flushinger, being ladened with the most part of the goods, saving the pepper; set sail for Lisbon, passing some small storms, not once meeting with any ship; but only on the [Portuguese] coast, where we saw ten Hollanders that sailed with corn towards Leghorn and other places in Italy: and so, by GOD's help! upon the 2nd of January 1592, we arrived in the river of Lisbon; being nine years after my departure from thence.

1592.

There I stayed till the month of July to despatch such things as I had to do: and upon the 17th of the same month, I went to Setubal; where certain Hollanders lay, with whom I went to Holland.

The 22nd of July, we set sail, being in all 12 ships; and because we had a contrary wind, we put out higher into the [*further out to*] sea.

The 27th of the same month, we had a lasting storm, whereby we ran against another ship; both being in a hundred dangers to be sunk, for we were within a span of touching one another: but GOD helped us, and we parted from each other; which almost seemed impossible. For the bore-sprite [*bow-sprit*] of the ship that came against us, strake upon our Fouke-yard; and therewith brake in pieces: and thereupon his Fouke-mast fell overboard; whereby he was forced to leave the fleet. Another also of our company had a leak, so that he made towards the [Portuguese] coast: where, to save the men, he ran the ship on shore; as, afterwards, we understood. So we remained but ten in company.

The 1st of August, being ninety miles in the [*out at*] sea, because the wind held contrary, so that we could not keep our right course; we espied three strange ships: but it was not long, before we lost the sight of them again.

The 4th of August, there came three other ships among our fleet, which we perceived to be Biscayens: whereupon we made towards them, and shot certain pieces at them; and so they left us.

The 16th of August, the wind being yet contrary, and because there were about fifteen passengers aboard our ship, our victuals, specially our drink, began to fail: so that we were constrained to keep an order, and to stint every man to his portion; being then 120 miles from Heissant [*Ushant*] inwards in the [*out at*] sea, which is called, the Half Sea.

The 18th, we had a storm, whereby three of our fleet were left behind; because they could not follow us.

The 24th of August we cast out the lead, and found ground; wherewith we were all glad, for it was the entrance into the Channel between England and France.

The 27th of August, being in the Channel, there came two small English ships to view our fleet, but presently put in again to the coast of England.

The 28th, we descried land, being loofward from us; which was Goutster and Dartmouth.

The next day, we passed by the Isle of Wight, sailing along the coast.

The 30th of August, we put into the head [Straits] of Dover and Calais; where there lay one of the Queen's ships; but she hoisted anchor, and sailed to the coast of England, without looking after us. So we set four men on shore [*i.e., in England*].

Then we had a scant wind, wherewith we entered into the North Sea; not seeing anybody.

The 1st of September, being cloudy, we had a storm out of the north-west, whereby we could not discern the land: but in the evening, we met with two ships that came out of the East Countries [*Baltic Provinces*], who told us they had seen land saying, "It was the Texel"; willing us to follow them. And so we discovered land, it being the Vlie: but we, thinking it to be the Texel, would not longer follow the other ships; but put so near unto it, that we were in great danger. Then we perceived that we had deceived ourselves, and saw the other ships take another course towards the Texel: but we had the wind so scant, and were fallen so low, that we could hardly get from the shore. And withal, we had a sudden storm, wherewith our Fouke-mast brake; our mainmast being already cracked: whereupon, we were fully determined to anchor there, and stand upon good comfort and hope in GOD. Suddenly the wind came better, so that with great pain and labour, about sun setting, we entered the mouth of the Texel, without any pilot: for, by reason of the great wind, they durst not come out. So, to conclude, we got in; and there, with thanksgiving to GOD, we anchored.

In the morning, being the 2nd of September, our Gunner thinking to charge the pieces, and, for joy, to shoot them off before the town: by fortune, a ladle full of powder took fire and, and with the fire thereof, strake off all his right hand, and burnt him in many places of his body; wherewith our joy was wholly quailed and abated.

The 3rd of September [*N.S.*], we arrived at Enkhuisen; where I found my mother, brother, and sister, all living and in good health: it being twelve years, nine months and a half, after my departure thence.

For which GOD Almighty, with His Son JESUS CHRIST our Saviour, be praised and blessed! To Whom belongeth all power, honour and glory, now and for evermore. Amen.

[Sir Richard Grenville's last words concluded: '*But the others of my company have done as traitors and dogs, for which they shall be reproached all their lives and leave a shameful name for ever.*']